Seven Secrets to the
Perfect Personal Essay

Also by Nancy Slonim Aronie

*Memoir as Medicine: The Healing Power of Writing Your Messy,
Imperfect, Unruly (but Gorgeously Yours) Life Story*

Writing from the Heart: Tapping the Power of Your Inner Voice

Seven Secrets to the Perfect Personal Essay

Crafting the Story Only *You* Can Write

Nancy Slonim Aronie

New World Library
Novato, California

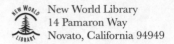 New World Library
14 Pamaron Way
Novato, California 94949

Text design by Megan Colman

Library of Congress Cataloging-in-Publication Data

Names: Aronie, Nancy Slonim, author.
Title: Seven secrets to the perfect personal essay : crafting the story only *you* can write / Nancy Slonim Aronie.
Description: Novato, California : New World Library, 2024. | Includes bibliographical references. | Summary: "A beloved writing teacher and essayist lays out the rules for crafting a remarkable personal essay, the kind that tells a story, moves readers, and reveals insights into the human condition — the kind that artificial intelligence can't write"-- Provided by publisher.
Identifiers: LCCN 2024026082 (print) | LCCN 2024026083 (ebook) | ISBN 9781608689309 (trade paperback) | ISBN 9781608689316 (epub)
Subjects: LCSH: Essay--Authorship. | English language--Rhetoric.
Classification: LCC PE1471 .A76 2024 (print) | LCC PE1471 (ebook) | DDC 808/.042--dc23/eng/20240614
LC record available at https://lccn.loc.gov/2024026082
LC ebook record available at https://lccn.loc.gov/2024026083

First printing, October 2024
ISBN 978-1-60868-930-9
Ebook ISBN 978-1-60868-931-6
Printed in Canada

10   9   8   7   6   5   4   3   2   1

New World Library is committed to protecting our natural environment. This book is made of material from well-managed FSC®-certified forests and other controlled sources.

MIX
Paper | Supporting
responsible forestry
FSC
www.fsc.org   FSC® C103567

For Joel

Contents

PART ONE

The *What*, the *Why*, and the *How*

So What Is a Personal Essay?

*B*asically, a personal essay is a description of an event or a situation told from your one-of-a-kind perspective. It's a story. It's a story about you and something else.

It is written in a conversational, intimate tone, using your voice, your language, your rhythms, your take. There is often a lesson, a teaching, a warning, an insight, a resolution.

Sometimes the ending is funny, sometimes it answers a question and reveals what you learned, sometimes it's a lecture.

Somewhere near the beginning, after you've introduced the topic, you must tell us how you screwed up or how you didn't know something or how you thought one way. And then as the essay unfolds, you realize there is another way of thinking, another way of going forward, a new way of looking at something. Something happens that becomes the solution or an answer to the problem you set up in the beginning.

What's the thing that changed your mind or switched you into this other way of seeing the situation? The essay relates your reflections on what actually happened.

An essential part of the personal essay, aka the personal narrative, is your willingness to be vulnerable. The reader has to relate to you and think, *Wow, you're just like me. I would have screwed up too.* When you admit you are not perfect, you give your reader permission to not be perfect too. Then they are on your team, cheering you on, and they become open-minded instead of judgmental.

In this kind of writing, you get to show your strengths and your resilience, your pain and your anxiety. It's mostly about you and your struggles, you and your challenges, you and your solutions, and you and your own personal growth.

What Can You Write About?

You can write about *anything*!!!

In the following pages you will find topics from the ridiculous to the silly to the intensely serious and maybe even to the sublime.

I have written about seeing a car hit my dog and sitting with her body while a cop came and gave me a ticket in the middle of a major walkway for having a dead dog in my lap.

I've written about driving my mother to the emergency room in the middle of the night and complaining that I was tired and annoyed that I'd been rudely awakened on a work night. And the guilt that followed. And finally realizing she was more important than sleep.

I have written about making myself learn how to use our complicated toilet paper holder — something that had always been my husband's job — as a survival skill so I wouldn't be lost in the event of potential widowhood.

Almost no subject is off-limits. What's fair game is any lesson you learned — how you got from point A to point L.

The best personal essays tell us how what happened and what you learned changed you. Don't worry if the changes are temporary. We all have insights and think, *Wow, I'm never gonna do that again. I get it now. I've been going down the wrong road all these years, and for the first time I see the error of my ways.* And we actually change our behavior for a week or a month or an hour. But then we become an asshole again. In other words, we are human, and we slide backward. We don't take catnaps; we take decade naps. But each time you have an insight, I say, *write about it!!!* You may regress, but by getting it down on the page, at least you pass on your momentary wisdom. And there it endures — right there, irrefutably on the page.

How Do You Get Your Ideas?

You can get ideas from everything and every place and every response you have to your own life experiences. Plenty of essays are about the eye-popping moments in life — the death of a loved one, abuse, travel mishaps, meeting a hero — and by all means, write about those if you're so inclined. But there's so much fodder to be mined in the mundane moments of everyday life.

For example, I'm a big eavesdropper. Sometimes when I hear someone say something, I have a strong reaction to it — something gets triggered — and I know I have the beginning of a piece. Or the ending. Or the middle. And I know not to waste it — it might as well go into words on the page. So I'll either write it down or say it into my phone. I know I won't remember it otherwise, and I also know I want it exactly the way I heard it.

Years ago when my kids were already grown-up, I was on the beach listening to the sounds of summer. I heard a little boy say, "Mama, how does the kite stay up?" I didn't hear an answer from the mother. Then I heard another little kid say, "Daddy, why do the dogs have to wear tags?" His father said, "Those dogs are gonna get into a fight — just watch. They shouldn't allow dogs on the beach."

Still another little one, who was digging a hole in the sand, asked something about China, and instead of answering, the mom said, "Now you've gotten your bathing suit all dirty."

I remember lying there thinking, *Why don't parents answer their kids?* which of course led me right to my own parenting. Did I listen? Was I half-present? Was I distracted? I went from my judgmental self of thinking these parents weren't doing their job to having total compassion and understanding of how hard it is to be constantly barraged with questions and what being a parent of small beings is like.

I wrote about it and taped it, and it aired on *All Things Considered* on NPR a few weeks later. So just an ordinary event with nothing exceptional happening can turn into an interesting essay with universal appeal.

A newspaper article, an argument with someone close, a cashmere sweater with moth holes. Anything is grist. The writing world is your oyster.

Oysters

Clams

A shrimp allergy

Allergy medicine

Allopathic healers

The Pittsburgh Steelers

Cucumber peelers

Arachnids with feelers

Las Vegas's top dealers

OK, NANCY, STOP!!!

How Long Should It Be?

The length can range from a few of the right words to billions of the right words. For comparison, a college essay should be four hundred to one thousand words, and essays for *The New Yorker* or *The Atlantic* run from two thousand to five thousand.

Don't worry about word count. Worry about meaning.

Actually, don't worry at all.

Sometimes students say to me, "But my story is too big," and I quote my friend and novelist Gerry Yukevich: "Writing a novel is like knitting a sweater for an octopus." Essays, on the other hand, are much less daunting, more like knitting a finger puppet. A lot less pressure! You're just giving yourself the task of writing about one particular episode from the vast tapestry of your life, in however many paragraphs or pages it takes. And who knows, if you write enough of them, eventually you might just have a garment worthy of a cephalopod.

How Do You Structure a Personal Essay?

In essence, a personal essay has three parts (and we'll cover this in more detail in Secret 6):

1. Introduction (the setup)
2. Body (the story)
3. Conclusion (the punch line)

Simple, really simple.

Pretend you're telling a friend about something that happened. You'd start at the beginning. *What's this about? What happened? Why am I telling you this?* You set it up. That's the introduction.

The body is the bulk of the story. All the details that are relevant, how you felt, where you were, who else was involved. What is actually happening. Your own unique perspective.

The conclusion is the aha moment, the realization that *Wait, it's not what I always thought it was. It's something totally different*:

> *Thank God I met that fourteen-year-old boy on the subway who told me about his mother.*
> Or *Thank the goddesses I scraped my brand-new car so I could have a little less judgment about people who have dents in their cars.*
> Or *If it weren't for all those rejections, I never would have learned the biggest lesson of my acting career.*

By the way, the realizations and the lessons don't have to be earth-shattering. They just have to be ego- or soul-enlightening.

Why Should You Write Personal Narratives?

As readers and humans, we are fascinated with story. We are hardwired to wonder about our fellow beings and what makes them tick...and yes, tic. "What happens next?" is programmed in everyone's psyche, whether it's conscious or subconscious. We want to know what's coming. Uncertainty is uncomfortable. And in an essay you get answers quicker than in real life or in longer forms of literature. It's a get-in-and-get-out kind of form, the perfect medium for our fragmented, overloaded twenty-first-century brains.

Essays are not linear, journalistic reports. They're your opinion, and no one can take that away from you. Readers may not agree with you, but they can't say, "I've fact-checked, and you're way off base."

In *Good Prose*, Tracy Kidder and Richard Todd wrote:

> Essayists tend to argue with themselves. The inner dialogue that might be suppressed in other writing finds a forum here. Montaigne blessed the form when he said, 'If I knew my own mind, I would not make essays, I would make decisions.'...When you write about your own ideas, you put yourself in a place that can feel less legitimate than the ground occupied by reporters or even by memoirists, who are, or ought to be, authorities on their subjects.

In other words, to write essays, you don't have to be an expert. You just have to be clear and have a trustworthy voice.

Half the time, I don't know what I feel until I write it. As Kidder and Todd write, "*How do I know what I mean until I hear what I say?*' is the familiar line. But the opposite is also true: How do I know what I *don't* mean until I hear what I say? Essays let you second-guess yourself, even contradict yourself in front of the reader. Self-doubt, fatal in so many enterprises, fortifies the essay."

So here's where you get to be the most you of you, the essence of you, the real you.

Your true self can never be wrong.

The root of the word *courage* is *coeur*. It means "heart" in French.

Your heart would never lie. It might exaggerate or romanticize, but it's on your team. So find that balance between heart and mind, invite your gut, tell passion to show up, use no restraint, and write your one-of-a-kind essay.

Come on. Have a heart.

Who Am I to Write This Book?

The first thing I ever got published was an essay on running — the only physical thing I had ever willed my body to do every day that my body did not want to do.

I had never had a discipline of any kind. When I took piano lessons, I quit at "Für Elise" because it required two hands. When I took Russian in college, I quit because I took up the whole blackboard trying to write one letter of the alphabet, and the professor said, "Meees Sloneem, you will never learn theees languitch." And when I was a baton twirler in high school (and dropped the baton more than I twirled it), the bandleader told me the only reason I was the head twirler was because I was tall. So I quit that too.

I grew up with a father who said, "Don't be a beginner. Beginners look ridiculous. Do what you're good at."

The translation of that bad advice was that looking accomplished was the most important value. So I learned early to do only what I was good at. That meant I had to find new people to impress, not new challenges to try.

The saddest part of my father's *misguidance* was that he had no idea what I would eventually learn from a pro — my husband: the deliciousness of what discipline feels like.

I married Joel, Mr. "I just want to get better at everything," and watched him make step-by-step progress not only with the violin but also with tennis and piano and cooking and gardening. When he took Suzuki method violin with our four-year-old, he walked around the house at all hours of the night and day playing "Twinkle, Twinkle, Little Star." He squeaked and screeched while I thought, *Why is he doing this? Doesn't he realize he's not good at it? He should quit.* And then one night he woke me up at 2:30 in the morning, whispering with reverence. He said, "Babe, babe, I made a breakthrough." It wasn't because I was half-asleep that I had no idea what he was talking about. It was because I had no idea what a breakthrough was. And he proceeded to play "Twinkle, Twinkle" smoothly, effortlessly, beautifully. No squeaking. No screeching. No quitting.

I sat and wept. How could I have reached this age and not known about practice, about process, about sticking to something? How could I not know about the benefit of doing something difficult? How could I even be a good parent? Who was I?

Running was the first thing I stuck to and the first thing I wrote about that got published. The connection is not lost on me. I was so in love with myself for sticking to this hard thing, got so high each morning from pushing myself out of bed into running gear and making myself get out the door, that I began to see a different person in the mirror. My cheeks were rosier, and my eyes were sparklier. And my heart, which I hadn't even known had been heavy, got lighter.

And then there were the woods, where for the first time I saw trees and talked to them. I smelled earth and stopped wearing perfume. I heard birds singing, and I heard crows arguing. Until those treks through the forest, I had always thought Mother Nature was someone else's mother.

I read somewhere that the root word of *discipline* is *disciple*, and, bolstered with my newfound confidence from running and from getting my story published, I began asking myself if I wanted to be the disciple of my own soul. On some level I knew my soul didn't come here exclusively to shop at Bloomingdale's for cashmere turtlenecks. I knew I had a higher purpose, although at the time, I never would have used those words. But seeing my husband as a role model — watching him get better at everything he tried by failing, picking himself up, dusting his sweet self off, and starting all over again — I started calling my writing "a writing practice." I forgave my father because we like to think our parents did the best they could. And after all, the poor guy never had his own role model, and who knows what bizarre messages he was given as a child.

After the piece about running got published in my local paper, I remembered something significant about my high school journalism class. I sat right in front of Mrs. Grenfell, my favorite English teacher. She would throw a blank piece of paper on my desk and say, "I need a piece on abortion and the law, nine hundred words." I would write it, and it would be in the school newspaper three days later with my byline. She did this every week for my whole senior year.

But until this piece about running was published, I had always thought the reason Mrs. Grenfell had given me all those assignments was because of where my desk was.

That is one low-self-esteem story, but it marked the birth of my writing career. Yes, career. In the forty-seven years since that running story, I have written for twenty-three publications, authored two (now three) books on writing, and read my essays on the radio as regular commentaries to NPR's *All Things Considered*. It turns out I am most comfortable with the essay form. Those nine-hundred-word assignments were the perfect training because when I started doing commentaries for NPR, they wanted only two minutes, and nine hundred words take two minutes to record. And I've been teaching writing for more than forty years. Since 1997, I have hosted the Chilmark Writing Workshops at my home studio on Martha's Vineyard, off the coast of Massachusetts, as well as workshops at other venues around the country. So I'm here to share the secrets I have learned along the way.

I am not an expert. I'm a writer with strong opinions. I don't have actual qualifications to teach essay writing. I didn't do research for this book. I didn't find information from esteemed essay writers to pass on to you. Most of what I've written when sharing what I think might be good advice for you is straight from my own experience, my own likes and dislikes, my own take on how to write a personal essay.

So take it all with a grain of salt.

But don't forget to add your own spices.

Silencing the Inner Critic
to Get Your Words on the Page

*D*iscipline may not be your problem. Confidence might be the block. Or comparing yourself to your favorite writer could be your nemesis. Or maybe it's a fear of putting yourself out there, revealing your deepest, darkest wounds for all the world to see.

One of the problems with writing an essay, and maybe writing anything, is your Uncle Max. Remember when he said, "You can't make money as a writer. Go to nursing school, honey"? Or your high school English teacher, who thought he was being funny when he held up your paper in front of the whole class and said, "Keep your day job"? Or just your own inner critic whispering, then yelling, "Who do you think you are? What, you've got something so interesting to say that everyone needs to hear it?" Or maybe your inner Eeyore tells you, "Everything's been said before, so why even try?"

Let's disarm these ogres one by one, shall we?

Nothing Compares to You

Who wants to follow Emerson or C. S. Lewis or Susan Sontag? Who wants to compete with James Baldwin and George Orwell? Who wants to come up against the likes of Alice Walker, Virginia Woolf, or Angela Davis? If I compared myself to Anna Quindlen, I'd never write another word.

Actually, I did try to get Anna Quindlen's job. It was 1994, and

I had just heard an interview with her on NPR. She announced she was leaving her coveted perch at *The New York Times*, where she had gained a huge national following for her column "Life in the Thirties." She was leaving because she wanted to write novels and be home with her kids. I didn't have any desire to write novels, and at that point I desperately wanted to be away from my kids.

So, after I turned off the radio, I gathered a bunch of my pieces that had aired on *All Things Considered* or been published in various newspaper Sunday magazines, put them in a big manila envelope, and addressed them to *Times* Executive Editor Abe Rosenthal.

In those days I swung between positively knowing that I would never be able to write another good sentence and having the balls to apply for Anna Quindlen's actual position at *The* (excuse me) *New York Times*.

One of the things I say over and over in the writing workshops I teach is, *"Don't compare yourself to ANYONE!!!"* So instead of measuring yourself to Zadie Smith or Mary Kerr or Flannery O'Connor (God knows I tried to be her for years), let your favorite one become your inspiration, your teacher, your muse. Read their work, and then sit down and write as a tribute to them.

Of course, when I go to write a new piece myself, I realize that not falling into the comparison well is easier said than done. When you feel yourself starting to slip is precisely when you block your ears or take a gummy or become your own dearest friend — and you sit down and write the damn thing.

Your Story Has Never Been Told

If you read an essay someone else wrote about being a kid whose mother died in a car wreck, and that's exactly what happened to you, it's foolishness to think there's no point in writing yours. No one else can write your story. No one else had your back porch with the loose step, no one else had your Aunt Esther with the space between her front teeth, no one else got bubble gum stuck in her braids and had all her hair cut off the day before her first day of sixth grade at a new school but you. No one else is you.

If you get intimidated, it will stop you. Don't stay in the shadows thinking, *Well, no one will be that interested.* How will you know if anyone would be interested if you never even put it into words?

I think it's safe to say that we've all either heard the question "Who do you think you are?" or "What makes you think anyone would care about your story?" or we've uttered it to ourselves. So many of us have been told "You're not good enough," "There's only so much to go around," "Only certain people get published," "You're not thin enough," "You're not pretty enough," and on and on. But what we all have in common is that little wise person in our bellies that, if we listen hard enough, we can hear say, *People will care. Yes, you are good enough. You are indeed. You are everything. You are the universe.* And the universe takes orders well. Now go write about whatever it is your unique personal history tells you to write.

If you need a little more of a mindset shift, go buy a Ganesh (remover of obstacles) to keep on your desk. Go pick out your outfit for your big meeting with your editor. Go rehearse your gratitude speech thanking your agent and your mother...and me.

Or just sit down and write.

Sharing Is Caring for Yourself

Essay writing is personal. Sharing what you think about a certain topic is risky. Especially if what you think is not what everyone else thinks. Writing an essay is like playing strip poker when you didn't wear enough layers so of course you keep losing.

Whether it's for school or work or because you have a response to something that's going on in your neighborhood, your town, or the world and you just want to get your take on it out there, you are going to be seen without your skivvies.

But revealing yourself in this way is a gift. You get to express your innermost thoughts rather than letting them marinate inside you in an imaginary conversational stew.

The thing to remember when you feel uncomfortable or insecure about coming out and letting people know who you really are is that the alternative is not good for the soul or the body.

Think about a nice piece of steak or fish or chicken or even asparagus or broccoli. When you marinate it and wait too long to cook it, it grows white fuzz. The meat actually becomes rancid, or the veggies get limp and slimy. I guarantee that if you don't get your pressing ideas out of your pancreas, your liver, or your heart, those organs will punish you for not letting your wisdom see the light of day.

Would you please just treat yourself the way you would your best friend? When you start doubting yourself and saying mean things to yourself, pretend you're your BFF and say nice things to cheer yourself on instead. My gramma used to say, "Play nice, children, play nice." So when you're being tough on yourself, I offer you her words: Play nice, play nice. 😄

At least write it. Then decide whether you want to share it with the world.

The Writing Gods Will Meet You Halfway

I have also learned that when you are willing to work, even if you only go halfway, the universe becomes your partner. If you're in the middle of writing a piece and you need the name of a river that begins with a P and has four syllables, the phone will ring, and your friend will breathlessly tell you about her Viking River Cruise down the Pilcomayo River. *Pil-co-ma-yo*. How does that happen? I'll tell you how it happens. The writing gods who live under your desk are watching all the time. You commit. They come out.

Oh and PS. I didn't get Anna's job.

No one did. She wasn't replaced.

AI and What Are You Gonna Do about It?

*B*y the time this book comes out, AI may have written a better one. There will probably be people who can read something and know immediately that it wasn't written by a person, those who won't know the difference, those who won't care, and those who are terrified and outraged.

Thinking about what AI will mean to the future of writing, I felt the impulse to write a book on how important essays are and to beg you all to not succumb to the ease of letting some artificial entity take your voice, use your voice, and then dull your voice. But then I let go of that impulse and thought, *Maybe AI will be a fad that fades into the land of the fax machine and those light-up kid sneakers.*

It's hard to know, given our addiction to technology. So I won't speculate. What I will do is talk about *soul*.

In the sixties, my sister became a devotee of Eckankar, a spiritual movement that teaches, among other things, the art of soul travel. Soul travel involves out-of-body experiences, but the soul, they say, doesn't actually go anywhere. Instead, soul travel is a natural ability that's a close cousin to dreaming. Anybody can do it. And that's because the soul is the unique innermost essence in every one of us. We just have to learn to tap into it.

Buddhists believe that *soul* refers to your inner life in relation to your own experience, as opposed to *spirit*, which is your inner life in relation to God. Soul is your mind, your heart, your will, and your imagination. It encompasses your thoughts, desires, passions, and dreams.

Hindus believe that all beings are souls and therefore spiritual in nature; that the body is temporary and eventually dies, but the soul is eternal; and that after death the soul is reincarnated, taking birth in another physical body.

I had a close girlfriend in high school who became a born-again Christian, and when I saw her at our ten-year reunion, she told me that because I'm Jewish, she prayed for my soul every day. I still loved her, so of course I thanked her. I mean, who am I not to take someone's genuine concern? Plus, her prayers might be working. I'm still kicking almost sixty years later.

So, *soul* has been defined and used and bandied about. It's one of those buzzwords that is now used to sell everything.

But personally, I can't put words to the word. It's a...feeling. Like, can you describe chocolate without using the word *chocolate*? But I know what I feel, and sometimes feelings just don't have sentences.

And when I read something written by ChatGPT, it's accurate and filled with facts but no chocolate. In other words, it lacks soul.

Essays are yours. They express your soul — your heart and mind and opinions and language and rhythms, your emotional connection to the topic. AI could never, ever do that.

So, what can you do about the AI invasion? Like anything new and shiny, you could start to worship it. But instead, use it for what it's best for, facts and info, but don't allow it to take your voice away. And don't let it abuse your particular brand of magic.

From Trauma to Triumph

After so many years of teaching writing workshops, sometimes I think I have heard everything. But of course, I haven't.

I heard about a cop who moved a dead body across the line of his jurisdiction so he could get home to his family for dinner, where he casually told them about it. The writer, the cop's daughter, was seven when it happened. She was fifty-seven when she wrote it.

I heard about a twelve-year-old girl whose mother was pregnant when her father died in a flaming plane crash. Her mother sent her to boarding school while she tried to take care of her new baby and steal a few moments to grieve. She remarried soon after, and the new husband had three daughters of his own. When the girl came home on vacations, she came home to a whole new configuration of family. Her room wasn't her room anymore. She now was forced to share it with twin girls five years younger.

She wrote the story when she was eighteen, and at the workshop the next summer, she brought her mother, who had never heard, never known, the trauma her daughter experienced. I got to watch the healing between them as they listened to each other's totally different sides of the same story. We all got to witness this absolutely beautiful softening of a relationship that had been struggling for years.

I watched and listened to a thirty-nine-year-old woman's written explanation of why she had never married. She wrote about the affair she'd been having with a married man since she was nineteen and how, because her lover was married, she had never told her mother, who was now sitting across from her in the same circle. I saw her mom jump out of her seat and hold her sobbing daughter, as the secret that had kept them apart evaporated like so much steam from a double boiler.

I've heard thousands of incest stories and hundreds of stories of fathers who said to their crying young sons, "If you don't stop that crying, I'll give you something to cry about." I've heard about mothers who made their kids sit at the table until they finished their lima beans, their liver, their milk — until midnight if necessary. I even heard one story recently where the kid said, "If I eat that I will throw up." The mother made her eat it, and she threw up. And the mother made her eat the throw-up. I've heard almost everything.

If you sat in on any of my writing workshops, and maybe most writing workshops, you might conclude that people shouldn't be allowed to have children until they pass a psychological test. But we all have heard, and some of us even say, "They did the best they could." I'm sure my kids would agree. It's a form of forgiveness, I suppose, but still, the wounds and the tiny murders that kids survive are actual traumas.

The definition of *trauma* from the Oxford dictionary is "a deeply distressing or disturbing experience." In order to survive day-to-day life, I think we tend to take all the bad stuff that happens to us and push the pain down as deep as we can. And we learn to function and look just fine. No one would know what happened at that kitchen table. But the by-product is, neither do we.

It's gone. The details are gone. The voices are gone. The memory is gone. But the wound is still there. Under the emotional spackling compound we've been using as a coping skill, there's the shard across our heart, there's the cut, there's the abuse. We paste a smile on our faces and move on. But underneath the sorrow, it's there rotting. I have said for years that pain is in our kidneys, in our pancreas, in our poor hearts. Putrefying. Poisoning. Polluting. At least get the story out onto the page. Don't worry — the details will come back. And if they don't, the exact color of the tablecloth isn't really what's important. How you *felt* about the event connected to the tablecloth is.

After decades of my guessing but feeling strongly about my theory, "narrative medicine" (the discipline of storytelling, which doctors have begun using to help diagnose and treat patients) comes along with actual data. Yes, sorrow and keeping your story inside affect your health. Telling or writing your story and having it be listened to, acknowledged, received is healing.

In my workshop what happens is the opposite of the parable of the blind man and the elephant. Because even though everyone's story is different (the trunk, the legs, the tail, the girth) the feelings are identical. Shame. Humiliation. Grief. Fear. No one is sitting in the sacred circle saying, "I don't get it." Rather, we're saying, "Holy shit, you too???"

Please understand that *trauma* doesn't necessarily mean you were raped, or you saw your father jump off a building, or you murdered your newborn. It's something that happened to you that was "deeply disturbing."

And *triumph* doesn't mean you won the lottery, you're on *The New York Times* bestseller list, or you met Prince/Princess Charming. It often means you have identified what happened to you and you have begun to connect the emotional dots and to look at how you can let go of the behaviors that have shaped you by that trauma.

Or maybe you did accomplish the almost impossible. You scraped off the hardened gypsum sulfate and glue and opened the wound, you bled, and you used a strong antibiotic cream, and some iodine. And this time, instead of letting it scab and scar, you used a Band-Aid to protect it and let it heal properly.

I'm remembering one of my millions of mini traumas. Fifth grade; spin the bottle. Donald Jacobsen and I go behind the curtain. This will be my first kiss. He's not even the boy I would have chosen, but still it's exciting and I'm all in. There is that awkward pause. I shut my eyes because I think that's what you're supposed to do. And then a whisper: "Let's just wait a few minutes and not do it."

That still stings after all this time. It went in somewhere. I'm not sure of its exact location. It's not as if I were walking around mourning that I got an early rejection. But where did that go? It didn't float away. It's lodged somewhere inside me like a splinter.

So how many of those did I accumulate before the self-esteem hard drive got filled and shut down the system? Writing is a great way to delete and make room.

Most effective of all is when you can get the blood on the page, while the trauma is fresh. I have always felt that when you're in the middle of trauma, writing something, anything, will have an immediacy to it that memory might not. The actual writing may not be your best, but the feeling will cut deeper.

And if I've said it once, I've said it a thousand, thousand times: Whatever you have endured, you can watercolor it, you can dance it, you can make little clay figures out of it, you can compose an opera with it, and in my workshop, you will write it. But the most important part of the equation is *first you have to feel it. You can't skip the pain part.* And you will notice, reading the essays in these pages, no one skipped the pain part.

Being willing to feel the heartbreak first, before you jump to the painting or the dancing or the sculpting or the composing, is the hard work. It means you must slog through the dark night of the soul or (in case you think there is no such thing as a soul) many nights and days and hours of deep sorrow. We live in a culture that says, "If you got a pain, we got a pill for ya." We don't really have models for grieving and sorrowing.

But if you do the slogging, the gift of doing this kind of hard work is — *ta-da!* — the healing.

Of course, you have to do the work. But so many of you are hard workers.

So be your own shrink and tell your client it's time. No more bitching and woe-is-me-ing. Tell her you'll be sitting front row center at her book signing.

Revising and Repurposing

One thing I love about the personal essay is that it's infinitely adaptable and customizable. You might think you've finished an essay, and then the next day you can read it again and realize you have more to say. Or less to say. Or maybe someone says something that you want to incorporate. Or maybe you want to submit it to a contest or publication but it's too long or too short.

So let's talk a bit about revision. I used to hate making changes after I finished writing something. Maybe because I'm lazy or because I fall in love with my own words and having to cut them is like killing off a blooming perennial in the garden. I always think I need all my original words.

But I have been lucky in that I was forced to learn how to edit. NPR wanted only two minutes, so editing myself was like working with a trainer at a verbal gym.

The biggest advance our civilization has ever made is the invention of the computer. Cut, Copy, and Paste (not to mention Undo) are miracles. You can go back. You can save. You can lift the sentences you loved from the first version. Oh, it's just an ADHD writer's dream.

You can see how the thing can get better. You can see what is no longer necessary. All my resistance to cutting anything melted when I finally learned how much better a piece could get. I didn't know that before.

The evolution of your story can be as extreme as an amoeba turning into a person. You might not even recognize what happened from the first draft to the finished piece.

I have gone from lazy and dreading to actually loving that work. But it took a long time. I know writers whose favorite part of writing is in the editing.

Just know that revision is part of the deal. And that your baby will be so much more powerful when it can walk and think and pick out its own clothes.

Then again, it may be that after long hours of work, you end up liking that first version. Sometimes you have to leave home in order to come back and appreciate what you had. Plus, even though I always say, "Don't write for your reader, write for yourself," when you have a specific assignment, you have to tailor the piece accordingly.

The bottom line: Unless you're highly unusual and the first draft is the perfect one, don't shirk the work.

To illustrate this, I thought I'd share four versions of the same story I wrote within five months of each other.

If anything, it will illuminate how you can write the same thing over and over and (a) it really does come out with big similarities; but (b) it also can change dramatically, depending on where you are emotionally at the time; and (c) the focus changes as you change as a person and depending on what specific venue you're writing for.

My Midlife Crisis (Midlife Is 83, Right?)

Version 1

How does one go from being apathetic to angry to fanatic? That was a rhetorical question. I don't have the answer. Maybe you do. But here's the story.

Growing up, there really wasn't much in the way of sports activity in my house. I had no brothers. Sports for girls in the fifties was a joke. Young ladies weren't supposed to sweat. Participating in an actual sport was as far from my reality as climbing Mount Everest barefoot in winter.

My father listened to baseball on the radio. And I do remember there was something comforting about the sounds of the announcer, Mel Allen, and the crack of a bat hitting a ball and the crowds cheering. It was a muffled background white-noise kind of thing, but now, in retrospect, the memory is really sweetly pleasant.

When I got married, my husband wasn't into sports either. He didn't know the NBA from the NFL. And I loved that about him. When the men would gather in groups at parties, the talk invariably would go to "How 'bout them Mets?" Joel didn't engage in those conversations, and often we would rehash the evening in the car on the way home. "What is it with guys who stay boys?" I would ask. "Why don't they talk about anything substantive?"

Then my husband started playing tennis in his fifties. And he started watching matches and YouTubes, and I watched as he threw himself into this new lifestyle. He had tennis buddies. He had games scheduled. He bought himself a bunch of rackets and spent more money on tennis balls than clothes and food and cars and...me. (OK, not me, but ya know.)

I had been swimming laps for some years now, so I guess sports, if you can call mine a sport, had slipped in surreptitiously. But I was certainly not one of those silly waste-of-time spectators.

But then my husband's three brothers who were all into watching basketball somehow recruited Joel into their web. I was almost tempted because I love these guys so much, but basketball? Uchh!

Then my husband started turning on the TV for Celtics games, which seemed to start in December and end in...well, never. And the noise from the TV began encroaching on my silence.

We live in a teeny cabin, so I had nowhere else to go. *What is going on?* I thought. *When did he start caring about this stupid sport?* I asked if he could watch with no volume, and he kindly put the thing on mute.

Then I don't know how I heard how much money these big players get, but when I heard, I had a conniption fit. I lost it. "Teachers," I yelled, "the most important profession there is, get nothing, make nothing, work their butts off, teach the future generation, and these assholes get a million times their salaries? It's obscene. It's wrong. It's f**ked up!!!"

Now comes the embarrassing part of the story. The "eating humble pie" part.

I can't even explain it. There is no logic to it. I can only say that by mistake one night, I looked up from my book and caught a glimpse of the dance on the screen. I couldn't take my eyes off it and found a whole different appreciation for what I had judged as men using sports as their only means of intimacy, a waste of productive time, and a desperate attachment to childhood nostalgia.

But here I was, mesmerized and moved. I said, "Babe, will you turn up the volume?" He was only too happy to comply. Now with the sound, I became even more engaged, glued to the TV. I don't know if it was the tribal thing, the belonging to something greater than, or the fact that now I had an excuse to call my brothers-in-law and scream into the phone, "No!!!" or "Yessss" or "I'm dying here!!!"

How does it happen that I know that I will jinx the game if I call too soon to celebrate when we're winning? (Please note: I just wrote "we're" referring to the Boston Celtics!!!)

I shape my evenings around the times the games are being played. I cancel dinner plans. I leave parties early. When I absolutely can't get away, I sneak looks at my phone to check on the score.

So there you have it. I have turned into a fan. A fanatic, in fact.

Just for your edification: I still think teachers are grossly underpaid. But I've made peace with the salaries of my boys, Jaylen and Jayson and Marcus and Derrick and Sam. And since I have a little crush on Marcus, I'm OK if he gets a bit of an increase. After all, I bet his hairstylist costs him a small fortune.

◆◆◆◆◆◆►

I wrote that piece for my column in *The Martha's Vineyard Times*. Besides my writing group and my husband, I don't usually send my columns to anyone prior to print. But since I've been watching the Celtics and sharing the ups and downs with my dear friend Richard, I sent it to him. He wrote back that he thought it was good but that he felt essays should have more substance, information, and quotes — and not just be a personal commentary.

So I took his advice and added some material that gave it a deeper look into being a fan. I kept the beginning part the same but changed everything starting from when I looked at the TV and first fell in love with the game.

Version 2

...I can't even explain it. There is no logic to it. I can only say that by mistake one night, I looked up from my book and caught a glimpse of the dance on the screen. I couldn't take my eyes off it. It was a ballet. These baskets they were making were not random acts. They weren't happy accidents. They were well rehearsed, the team a human machine, well oiled and flawless. I was watching anticipation and intuition and communication. I was watching the result of millions of hours of practice — which, it turns out, does make perfect.

So what happened? I found a whole different appreciation for what I had judged as men using sports as their only means of intimacy, a waste of productive time, and a desperate attachment to childhood nostalgia.

I was mesmerized and moved. I asked my husband to turn up

the volume. He was only too happy to comply. With the sound, I became even more engaged, glued to the TV. I don't know if it was the tribal thing, the belonging to something greater than, or the fact that now I had an excuse to call my brothers-in-law and scream into the phone, "No!!!" or "Yessss!" or "I'm dying here!!!"

I began to shape my evenings around the time of the games. I canceled dinner plans. I left parties early. When I should have been listening to someone talk, I snuck looks at my phone to check on the score. What was happening to me? No one seemed to worry about me. If anything, I was getting rewarded for my complete immersion in this bizarre culture, loving and caring about anything to do with the Boston Celtics.

I worried that maybe being a fan was getting out of hand to the point of distraction. I'm not gonna say I stopped making my husband's dinners or washing my underwear or started running out of gas on the highway, but short of those things, I was hooked.

I wondered if I should join Sports Fanatics Anonymous (is there such a thing?), so I googled "sports watching addiction." What did I discover? One article in *Psychology Today* reported, "For many, watching sports is seen as a sad and dangerous waste of time." But luckily I kept reading and found:

> Being a sports fan, it turns out, can bring about a good deal of joy and well-being into people's lives.
>
> In their recently published textbook *Sport Fans: The Psychology and Social Impact of Fandom*, Drs. Daniel L. Wann and Jeffrey D. James, professors at Murray and Florida State University, have documented the growing evidence for sports fandom's benefits. Being identified with a sports team is reliably related to higher levels of happiness, well-being, and even meaning in life, they report.
>
> But how can something as seemingly trivial as being a sports fan contribute to well-being? Part of the answer may lie in how it connects us with others. Like other sorts

of social institutions, sports offer people a reason to come together. A reason to talk up a stranger at a bar. A reason to gather the family for a Sunday night ritual. A reason to message an old friend when your team finally starts playing well.

Well, then there ya go! I knew I was having a great deal of joy and well-being. Otherwise how could I have been ecstatically jumping up and down alone in my own house yelling, "Go Celts!!!"

I still think teachers are grossly underpaid. But now that I know I'm not on the edge and I have plenty of company in my new passion, I've made peace with the salaries of my guys, Jaylen and Jayson and Marcus and Derrick and Sam. And since I have a little crush on Marcus, I'm OK if he gets a bit of an increase. After all, I bet his hairstylist costs him a small fortune.

◗◖◖◗◗◖◗►

The Celtics GM has since broken my heart by trading my guy Marcus Smart to the Memphis Whatevers, ruining the cute ending I labored over. Oh well, another opportunity for revision.

Then, five months later, my brother-in-law died, and the whole idea of watching the Celtics became a brand-new step into emotional bravery and courage and a life-must-go-on kind of deal. Revising the essay again became a hugely helpful step in my grieving process.

Version 3

When I got married, my husband wasn't into sports, playing or watching. He didn't know the NBA from the NFL. And I loved that about him. When the men would gather in groups at parties, the talk invariably would go to "How 'bout them Mets?" Joel didn't engage in those conversations, and often we would rehash the evening in the car on the way home. "What is it with guys who stay boys?" I would ask. "Why don't they talk about anything substantive?"

But his youngest brother, Mart, who was nineteen when I met him, was a Celtics diehard. I loved this guy, and we were very close in the early years of my marriage. But I had kids and he got into an edgy lifestyle, and somehow I lost him.

When my husband started playing tennis in his fifties, he started watching matches and YouTubes, and I watched as he threw himself into this new hobby. He had tennis buddies. He had games scheduled. He bought himself a bunch of rackets and spent more money on tennis balls than clothes and food and cars and...me (OK, not me).

Once Joel started on the jock path, it was easy for his three brothers, who were all into watching basketball, to recruit my husband into their web.

But I was certainly not one of those silly waste-of-time spectators.

All of a sudden the TV was on for NBA games, which seemed to start in October and end in...well, never. And the noise from that television began encroaching on my silence.

I asked if he could watch with no volume, and he kindly put the thing on mute.

Then the phone calls started. The brothers yelling into the phone, "Nooooo! Did you see that? That wasn't a foul, you idiot! He barely touched him!" They were watching in unison in two different time zones and four different locations.

I can't explain what happened. There is no logic to it. I can only say that by mistake, one night, hearing the nonstop dialogue from the speakerphone, I looked up from my book and caught a glimpse of the dance on the screen. I couldn't take my eyes off it. It was a ballet. These baskets they were making were not random, surprising acts. They weren't happy accidents. They were well rehearsed, a human machine well oiled and flawless. I was watching anticipation and intuition and communication. I was watching the result of millions of hours of practice — which, it turns out, does make perfect.

I began to find a whole different appreciation for what I had judged as men using sports as their only means of intimacy, a waste of productive time, and a desperate attachment to childhood nostalgia.

I was mesmerized and moved. I asked my husband to turn up the volume. He was only too happy to comply. With the sound, I became even more engaged, glued to the TV. I don't know if it was the tribal thing, the belonging to something greater than, or the fact that now I had an excuse to connect with Mart and scream into the phone, "No!!!" or "Yessss" or "I'm dying here!!!"

And it was Mart, the best athlete of the bros and the commentator for the new family sports channel, who penetrated my consciousness first with his admonishment of "Don't jinx it, Nance, don't jinx it," when I called to celebrate a win before the game was over.

I began to shape my evenings around the time of the games. I canceled dinner plans. I left parties early. I started sneaking looks at my phone to check on the score when I should have been listening to someone talk.

And then my Mart got sick. He was diagnosed with throat cancer, and it became harder and harder to understand him on the phone. We still called each other, but between my constantly saying, "What?? Say that again, sweetie," and screaming when Tatum made a three pointer, the thing started losing its joy.

Mart died three months ago, and the Celtics season started up that same week. I couldn't turn on my TV. The remaining three brothers started up with the calls. They said the team never looked this good. "Something shifted," they said. "It's otherworldly," they said. "You won't believe Derrick White. He can't miss!! And Jaylen! Oh my God!!! And now they've got this guy Porziņģis. He's seven-two!!!"

"Nance," they yelled, "where are you?" I didn't know where I was.

And then it came to me. This was grief.

It wasn't just the game that had drawn me in. It was the reconnection with my precious brother-in-law. And now that was broken, and I couldn't imagine caring anymore.

I've learned grief. I know it. I know how to navigate feeling sorrow and recovering. But somehow, I had forgotten. You don't throw the baby out with the bathwater. You keep the baby. You change the bathwater. But first you mourn. You honor the pain part. And I was trying to skip the pain by shutting off the TV.

So this Friday night at 7:30, with trepidation and a willingness to feel my broken heart, I will return to my team and scream on Mart's behalf. "Don't jinx it! Don't jinx it." Don't worry, Mart, I won't.

And here's version 4, which I wrote for a radio show whose maximum word count was 450. This is 366.

Version 4

When I got married, my husband didn't know the NBA from the NFL. And I loved that about him. But Mart, my youngest brother-in-law, was a Celtics diehard. I loved this guy, but over the years, our connection faded.

All three of my brothers-in-law were into basketball, and they ultimately recruited my husband into their web. In recent years, their phone calls were peppered with "You idiot — that wasn't a foul!" and "Tatum, I love you!!!"

One night, I caught a glimpse of the dance on the screen, and my resistance to what I'd felt was boys who never grew up melted. It was pure ballet. These baskets they were making weren't happy accidents. These guys were human machines, well oiled and flawless. I was watching a kind of genius.

Suddenly I was hooked. I don't know if it was the tribal thing, the belonging to something greater than, or the fact that now I had Mart back in my life and I could scream into the phone, "No!!!" or "OMG" or "I'm dying here!" When I called to celebrate a win before the game was over, Mart lovingly corrected me: "Don't jinx it, Nance, don't jinx it!"

And then my Mart got sick. He was diagnosed with throat cancer, and it became harder and harder to understand him on the phone.

Mart died three months ago, and I couldn't watch the games. But the other brothers continued their calls.

"Nance," they yelled, "where are you?" I didn't know where I was.

And then it came to me. It wasn't just the game that had seduced me. It was the reconnection with my precious brother-in-law And now that was broken, and I couldn't imagine caring anymore.

This was grief. I know grief.

You don't throw the baby out with the bathwater. You keep the baby. You change the bathwater. But first you mourn. You honor the pain part. And I was trying to skip the pain by not watching anymore.

So this Friday night at 7:30, with trepidation and a willingness to feel my broken heart, I will return to his team and scream on Mart's behalf.

And don't worry, Mart, I won't jinx it.

How to Use This Book

So now you have a few hints as to what's expected in an essay written with your opinion, your perspective, your worldview. The crucial part is the teaching you will pass on to your reader, who doesn't simply want to be entertained but is hungry for your sage slice of life.

And the rest of this book is devoted to giving you lots more hints in the form of my seven secrets to writing the perfect personal essay. Each of the remaining chapters reveals one of those hard-won secrets. It begins with a few insights on the subject from yours truly, but in the spirit of the tried-and-true writing advice of "show, don't tell," the meat of it is a selection of essays that exemplify that particular secret.

Most of the essays were written by students in my workshops, either on the spot or as "homework" in response to a nightly prompt. Some of them were written in fifteen minutes right in class ("Bellowing the Truth" by DeDe Lahman on page 171 is one example). Most of the writers are regular people trying to make sense of their lives, and many have gone on to have their essays published. You can find their bios at the back of the book. When you have read the work in these pages, it will support my theory that writing your story can take the tiny murders that happened to you and turn them into gold.

Each essay is followed by a writing prompt designed to help you keep going. You won't be able to moan to anybody, "I can't think of anything to write." If I hear one of you say that, I'm coming to your house personally. I'm gonna sit you down and hand you a legal pad and a really good Pilot pen.

After the first essay in each chapter I will make my comments as if we were in the sacred circle in my studio in Chilmark. The things I say are about the things I love. They are not necessarily what an editor or an agent or other readers would love. I am not an "expert." I am responding to what moves me. So my take shouldn't be taken as gospel. It's my own personal taste.

I think we live in a withholding society (especially here in New England), and people tend to think they are either supposed to tell you what's wrong or not speak up at all. And since by nature I am hyperbolic, all I do in the workshop is model how to gush appropriately. At the end of the workshops I joke, "I don't teach writing; I teach gushing." See if you think these essays are gush-worthy as well.

Read the essays and advice. Enjoy! And then…go write your own!

No pressure. You don't have to, but I mean, you have this book. You might as well use it.

Besides, if you toss it in the bin or shelve it in some obscure place in your den, it will know.

Books have feelings too.

This book is designed to stop you from procrastinating on writing your own stellar personal narrative or a collection of them. If one more person says, "You should write that," tell them, "Thank you. I will!"

PART TWO

The Seven Secrets

Start with a Compelling First Statement

(Or, in My Vernacular: Kill 'Em with the First Line)

*T*he first sentence has to grab the reader. Otherwise, you will probably lose them. Even if seven seconds later you shine, that'll be seven seconds too late.

That first sentence is the hook. It's the only way to get the reader's immediate attention and draw them into the essay. It sets the tone for the entire story and gets your reader to keep going.

I was an editor once, and I know what it's like to have a bunch of manuscripts on your desk waiting. If I didn't flip over that first line, I'm sad to say I moved on. I always felt as if I were in a rush to find the best piece possible.

Your opener has to have an immediacy about it. It's got to have original phrasing. It can't have any clichés. I think clichés are fine elsewhere in essays, but not in that opening sentence.

It can be long. It can be short. It can be funny. It can be maudlin. It just has to have the right rhythm, the right word choices, and not sound like anything you've ever read before.

Mark Nepo, in *The Book of Awakening*, begins an essay with: "Many of us are raised by well-intending parents to be the carriers of their sadness." This works because it's so universal.

Molly Ivins, the political columnist who often wrote for *The Nation*, began one of her many essays with: "Nothing like a Republican convention to drive you screaming back into the arms of the Democrats." Funny. I'm in. I want more.

In Virginia Woolf's *On Being Ill*, she writes this opening sentence:

> Considering how common illness is, how tremendous the spiritual change that it brings, how astonishing, when the lights of health go down, the undiscovered countries that are then disclosed, what wastes and deserts of the soul a slight attack of influenza brings to view, what precipices and lawns sprinkled with bright flowers a little rise of temperature reveals, what ancient and obdurate oaks are uprooted in us by the act of sickness, how we go down into the pit of death and feel the waters of annihilation close above our heads and wake thinking to find ourselves in the presence of the angels and the harpers when we have a tooth out and come to the surface in the dentist's arm-chair and confuse his "Rinse the mouth — rinse the mouth" with the greeting of the Deity stooping from the floor of Heaven to welcome us — when we think of this, as we are so frequently forced to think of it, it becomes strange indeed that illness has not taken its place with love and battle and jealousy among the prime themes of literature.

OMG! So that's Virginia Woolf. No wonder she needed a room of her own. (Kidding.) Only Virginia and James Joyce can go on and on like that. The rest of us had better read that first sentence over and over and make sure every word is necessary.

Laura Lentz, one of my favorite writers, began one of her essays with the following: "Years ago, when I was deep in a relationship with my first love, who would die four years after we met, I was a hummingbird living in an intoxicating city."

"I was a hummingbird." Yum!

Anne Lamott, the most brilliant of us all, started one of her essays in *Dusk, Night, Dawn* with this winner: "I continue to wait patiently for several people to come to me begging for my forgiveness before they die — a change that is about as likely to happen for me as any breakthrough for the turkey in the old *New Yorker* cartoon marching with a placard that says 'Repent!' " Lamott's humor reels us in, but her underlying message is what makes us want more. You know she is going to deliver both the laughs and the wisdom.

What we want most is originality.

So, start with an original blue-chip opener. Here are some of my favorite examples from some of my favorite students (*oh, come, Nancy, you know they're all your favorites*) in my workshops over the years.

Exit Now

Jan Cook Chapman

In the way old days — long before small-town hospitals and highways looked easily matched in their concrete and brick clothes — I took my first breath in a hospital room that cozied up alongside a busy Tennessee highway. Surely, among coos of parents and clatters of medical things in those first days, there was traffic noise. The moan and whine of lumbering trucks, speeding cars, emergency vehicles. The hum of rubber on road. I believe strongly (though the belief may not be scientifically sound) that visceral auditory birth memory stays with us, and I use that origin story to explain why life only makes sense to me — really — in the context of a good highway analogy. The speed, the crazy turns, the unpredictable drivers in our lanes. The journey, the wandering off the beaten path, the signs. Every writer has written something about The Road. And it hits a home run with me every time.

Lately, though, I've been weirdly focused on exit ramps rather than stretches of striped concrete that poetically end at the horizon no matter how far you go. Most of us recognize and scoot off the highway of life at the planned exits: childhood, formal education, long-time careers. If we've lived well on The Road, we've had to swerve to take an unplanned exit or two — from a relationship, a treasured dream, a definition of perfection. But what about those sign-heralded, slanted-arrow invitations we race past when perhaps we shouldn't? The exits not taken. How do they define the journey?

I may have missed an important exit over forty years ago, in a time when phrases like *PTSD* and *trauma therapy* were yet to inhabit the vernacular. I was a married woman of twenty-four, living with my university student husband in the best place one hundred dollars a month could buy. I had landed a big new job in a TV newsroom and felt on top of the world as I spent a solo Tuesday evening sewing a new dress to wear to my first day on the job. Husband-at-the-library was an every-night requirement of our four-hundred-square-foot efficiency plus kitchen space, tucked behind the home of a dear widow. I was alone in that little apartment until bedtime nearly every evening.

We knew the place had been noticed by someone interested in our stuff. A bicycle had been taken, a gate had been left open, and we'd had the feeling the times of our comings and goings were known by a stranger. But bad things didn't happen to kids like us. The incidents were noted. Shoulders were shrugged. We marched on.

Until that Tuesday evening.

That night, as I pinned and cut pattern on fabric on the bedroom side of the wall that separated our bedroom, the only door into the space opened, and I heard a male voice I didn't know say, "Hello?" There was no question I was in trouble. And there was no way out. My brain went into emergency operations mode, quickly instructing my heart to pound furiously just below my vocal cords while telling my shaking legs to carry me two steps around the edge of that room divider so I could face the intruder with scissors in hand and scream, "Get out!"

I learned a couple of things that night. Scissors are a bad idea if you're not strong enough to hold on to them. They can be taken and used against you. I have two scars only I see anymore. One is on my hand, the other on my neck. I find the one at the base of my left index finger and rub it every time I hear of a woman attacked by an intruder or see a rape scene in a movie or find myself within earshot of an angry, yelling man. In those moments, my heart instantly roars into place at the bottom of my throat, and I blink fiercely to push everything but the scar from my memory.

I also learned that night that you cannot bargain your way clear of evil. Once it's in your house, about all you can do is survive it.

Beyond that, I learned that locking doors can be a good idea. I am beginning to wonder what else I should have carried with me from that violent attack so many years ago.

At the time, the road of emotional numbness was littered with the distractions of a hospital visit to confirm the trauma; a consult with victim's advocates, who laid out the potential terror of taking a rapist to court; and a befuddling stop at the police station to look through mug shots. Then life went on. There was a new job to learn, a semester of school to finish, one hundred dollars of rent to be paid. If there was an exit ramp on that fast-moving highway, we missed it. Big-time.

So now, as I find myself mostly driving in the slow lane, I've begun to wonder about that exit I sped past so long ago. Too long ago, really, to find the mile marker and wander off the highway. But I have questions.

What was off that exit ramp? A place to rest and think about how my life, my early marriage, my hopes for the future had changed? How I had changed? Might there have been a moment of awareness whenever broken trust or strangers or sudden change shifted my soul into a pit stop of fear and trembling? Could someone have warned me I might lose all ability to remember things I see as I shut down, over and over again, when remembering the horror of that one scene?

How different might the entire trip of my life have been if I'd slowed down to read the signs so brilliantly placed in mile, half-mile, quarter-mile increments to tell me: *Slow down. Change lanes. Refuel. Stretch. Grab a snack. Check the map. Then, only then, get back on the road.*

"*Still round the corner there may wait / a new road or a secret gate.*"

— *J. R. R. Tolkien*

My Take

I love the opening. It pulls me in immediately. The extended metaphor of the highway works. "The exits not taken" is foretelling. Which exits did the writer not take?

I love numbers, since they are such good details. She has twenty-four (her age), one hundred dollars (the rent), and four hundred square feet (the apartment).

"I was alone" starts to make me a bit nervous, but I'm OK until she writes about the bicycle and the gate. Now I'm on full alert.

"Noted," "shrugged," "marched" — crisp verbs all ending in *-ed*. Gorgeous sound.

That separate sentence, all by itself, "Until that Tuesday evening" is chilling. Now I'm on fuller alert.

"No question" and "no way out" — nice balance.

"Instructing," "telling," "shaking" — nice trio of *-ing*s.

When she mentions the scissors, we feel, "Oh good, she's got a weapon." But then with "I learned a couple of things that night," she reveals that the scissors were not so good.

The scars show, not tell, us what happened. She reveals the trauma incrementally by specifically naming the locations of the scars (hand and neck) and then by listing the three triggers that cause her to rub the scar at the base of her left index finger.

I love the line "I blink fiercely to push everything but the scar from my memory."

When I read "you cannot bargain your way clear of evil," I can hear her trying to survive by maybe offering him whatever he wants.

"Once it's in your house" makes evil a character.

With "the road of emotional numbness," she reveals the truth that trauma can make you numb.

"Then life went on. There was a new job to learn, a semester of school to finish, one hundred dollars of rent to be paid." So yeah, you know life does go on, but now life is very different. The writer has been wounded. The writer is changed. The writer is beating herself up for missing the exit ramp.

Here is where our hearts hurt for the writer. Vulnerability is a key element in a personal essay (see Secret 4). And she is an innocent victim. Instead of complaining, she is blaming herself while she is learning for the future.

But her innocence is gone. She won't be leaving her metaphoric door open again.

Her ending, with the wisdom she has gained, is just so powerful: "*Slow down. Change lanes. Refuel. Stretch. Grab a snack. Check the map. Then, only then, get back on the road.*"

 PROMPT: Write a piece on missing an important exit.

A Holy Bagel

Peter Meyer

There I sat, as far from the altar, the priest, and that wafer as I could. To my right sat my girlfriend and her sweet and authentic family, even though, *Shhhh! I'm a Jew being held temporarily captive in a church for Christmas Mass!* To my left sat true believers listening intently to the word of God. I steadfastly ignored them.

After some quite-decent singing (this was an Episcopalian

church, after all) and a not-too-strident sermon, everyone in that surreal space stood up and strode to the front to receive Communion, to consume the corporeal Christ — to ingest the body of *the* guy! Apparently, taking in the piece of holy bread, which Laurie had told me earlier was actually called "the Eucharist," was the pinnacle of the congregation's display of commitment to their faith, a most holy and sacred sacrament. The mass of humans moving together was impressive in its unity but also terrifying in its immediate ability to clearly separate the pious from the pretenders, the invited from the intruders. To me, it seemed clear that any sitters would stand out as the sinners. So I stared, stunned, frozen in the frenzied panic of the moment. In my warped and twisted mind, I imagined the parishioners as hippies lining up, then kneeling to take a hit of acid on a hot Central Park night. Some distorted mash-up of *Dark Side of the Moon*, "Strawberry Fields," "Within You Without You," and "Black Magic Woman" played internally as a backdrop to this surreal scene surrounding me. Where was this trip taking them? My mind wandered in the swirling haze of Our Fathers and other church mumbo jumbo.

Then suddenly, the psychedelic cinema projecting onto the walls of my cranium stopped abruptly, holy hymns replacing the kaleidoscopic soundtrack, and I was overcome with an intense urge to bolt. But I was also tempted to take the easy bait and bluff. I could just take a few innocent paces to the front and bend, pretending that I wasn't the sole disbeliever (or at least agnostic). I'd pose as if I belonged here in this place with these people. I'd then walk back to my pew and kneel, head bowed, as though giving thanks in pious prayer for the privilege of having ingested the flesh of their Lord. I thought to myself, "When Laurie asked me just last week what superpower I wanted, why didn't I say, 'invisibility'?!"

However, in my paralysis, instead of performing the scene I'd rehearsed in my head just seconds before and walking up the aisle with the others like a zombie from *Dawn of the Dead*, or at least sneaking out for a fake emergency bathroom trip, I found myself sitting my ground and staying put in my pew. I was shocked at my resolve. That instinct, alien to me then, of integrity and guts, had grabbed hold. I felt a brief burst of trust that I wouldn't die in that moment, exposed as a heathen, cast up on a cross or even stoned to death.

However, I was young, and my fresh and tentative bravery had its limits. "Why didn't you take the Communion?" a shrill and nasal voice to my left inquired in quite a forward fashion, interrupting my internal celebration of newfound determination.

What the hell? Get off my case, you nosy Christian soldier, I thought to myself. But the next words that came out of my mouth instead shocked me. I blurted out, "I'm just not hungry right now," surprised by the gumption running counter to my usually shy and conflict-avoidant self.

The look of shock and revulsion on this intrusive woman's flushing face was worth all the tightening limbs, all the tensioning and lifting of my shoulders, all the escalating emotional discomforts I'd endured in the moments just prior. Right then, I began to see that all moments, even difficult ones, do pass. In the grand scheme of things, the discomfort is transient, fleeting, even teaching. There is no forever Pause button; the film eventually spins forward. And it ends, whether in tragedy or happily ever after.

When we were packed in the minivan shortly after, my retelling of that moment provoked a priceless chorus of belly laughs and giggles, sending us all into the evening in a lighthearted and joyful spirit as we strode toward the sunset in what had turned out to be happily ever after. It was not a tragedy at all. With Laurie's family, I had not betrayed myself, yet I revealed the limits of my bravery. And even so, I was not rejected, torn to shreds, or strung up on the gallows.

At the same time, perhaps a spirit of love had found me in that lovely church full of good people after all. I had found new courage, heard early whispers of trust, maybe even begun to let my soul stir. And perhaps I was more honest and direct than I had realized. Back then, I *wasn't* hungry for a spiritual life yet; *it* was pursuing *me*, patiently tapping me on the shoulder year after year, waiting for when I would be ready to bake my own holy bread. Spirit moves in mysterious ways. Maybe the mystics, the wafer eaters, the Jews, and the acid hippies, in unconscious communion, were all after the same thing.

To this day I wonder how that wafer would taste with some nice smooth cream cheese slathered over it, topped with a little lox. I don't think there's enough real estate on that cracker for onions and capers, though.

 PROMPT: Was there ever a time you felt a spiritual life was pursuing you?

Dinner at Our House Was…

Suzanne A. Seggerman

Hurl the caviar bowl across the room so the black slop slithers down the wall like drying blood, fling the smoked salmon and the toast points until they slap their wet slime on the grand piano, wipe the champagne flutes off their mirrored tray with one broad swipe of the arm, like a knife severing the top of a gourd.

And then crank off the volume on the crackle of laughter, born of a thousand years of shared trauma, the bespoke humor of our known and specific pain, our secret language of irony and shame, exuberance and loss. For only we know the same sorrows, the same tongue curled around our dysfunction and despair. Shut it all off, shut it down, for I no longer want to hear you, have you in my body, no longer want the slightest light slipping through.

I am done with you, all of you, for your avarice and vice, your viciousness and human debasement. How can I call you my flesh and blood, my bones and nerve endings, the places of slack and vulnerability, when you have clawed my life from me? Clawed from me my home, my refuge, the sweet fortress of safety, built from years of the plasterwork of real love, the bulwark of stability, kindness, the kindness of my family, my real family, the one forged from unblood, forged with intention, the careful coiling of seeing and knowing one another, of affirmation and animation. On our kitchen counter, let the cups be anchored to their saucers, the plates fixed in place. Bowls of hot oatmeal, buttered noodles, supermarket chicken encased in its plastic cage, may they lay rooted, the hands reached across the table, steady as a morning rain, holding each other, never letting go.

 PROMPT: Write an angry piece about a family member.

A Love Affair with Kale and Feta
(Or, Everything Tastes Betta with Feta)

Catherine Walthers

I have to apologize up front for my overuse of feta.

Overuse of an ingredient has happened in my other cookbooks. In the soup book, it was leeks. At one point I realized that I used leeks in almost every soup. Leeks add another level of flavor beyond onions. But did nearly every soup need one? The very first soup I made in high school was potato leek, and I still love that combination and have made countless variations, including the cream of kale soup in this new book, *Kale, Glorious Kale*. Farro was another discovery. I thoroughly enjoy the toothiness of farro instead of barley and created a chicken farro soup, a beef and farro soup, and even a kale farro soup. All delicious. But I had to force myself to stop — what if someone doesn't like farro or can't locate it in their grocery store?

About three months into writing *Kale, Glorious Kale*, I searched the word *feta* in my manuscript to find a specific recipe, and I realized it was happening again. Feta came up at least seven times. It made me a little sad because I was only halfway into testing recipes — what if feta would turn out to be perfect for another recipe?

Let's see. I had three dinner salads with baby kale, varied vegetables, and some with fish or chicken. All had feta. The breakfast casserole combined eggs, kale, onions, and feta. Oh, there were two egg and kale dishes with feta. Of course, I would add feta to the Greek greens dish spanakopita, now kale-kopita. And delicious, I might add.

Kale and feta taste great together. The slight saltiness and wonderful flavor of feta elevate kale, which needs salt and boosting complementary flavors. If you are ever wondering what cheese to use in a kale side dish or especially a salad, think no further.

As an aside, here's a word or two about feta in general: Not all types are created equal. I think that's the case with many foods. Some fetas can be too salty. Some have little flavor. Feta can be different depending on whether it's made from cow's milk, goat's milk, or sheep's milk. And textures can vary.

Those made with sheep's milk are favorites, especially those made in France — including a Valbreso feta — and in Greece, among other European countries. The Greek often combine sheep's and goat's milk for some wonderful feta. I don't always love goat's milk alone — like goat cheese, it can taste too strong — but as part of a feta, it works.

I saw an inexpensive Bulgarian feta in bulk at the local supermarket one day and thought I could save some money in my testing. It was too strong and changed the whole flavor of the dish.

Cookbooks often reflect the likes and dislikes of the author. I noticed a whole chapter devoted to eggplant in Yotam Ottolenghi's book *Plenty*, a cookbook I was enjoying cooking from. But I haven't tried any of those recipes because I'm not an eggplant fan. And this is the price one can pay — everyone has different tastes. You might find one eggplant recipe in all four of my books. I don't love green peppers either, and rarely use them.

I had to laugh that two guest recipes in this book also happened to have, you guessed it, feta. One is a kale salad that won the local kale fest. And to be fair, its creator is a cheesemaker who had made the feta. The other is a great combination of kale, farro, apple, dill, and feta.

Other cheeses do go well with kale, for the same reason feta works: the slight saltiness, the richness, and the overall flavor it brings to the earthy kale. Parmesan and kale taste delicious — on salads and in kale pesto. In fact, kale has an affinity with many cheeses, including blue cheese, goat cheese, and cheddar. A friend who was recently living in Switzerland suggested Gruyère, having used it on her potato leek soup. I tried it with my kale soup with potatoes and leeks and understood her choice. So now, whenever I notice my fixation with feta and kale, I actively think, *Can this work with another cheese?*

While I'm at it, I should also apologize for probably having too much fruit in the book. I love all fruit. And I can't help it that fruit also tastes delicious with kale. Kale benefits from a touch of sweetness, especially in salads and smoothies. A few raisins, a juicy peach, apples, grapefruit, oranges, pineapple, mango, blueberries, dates, figs, plums, grapes, and so on. There's a great spring salad using a simple combination of baby kale, fresh strawberries, and feta...I mean goat cheese.

 ► **PROMPT:** Write a piece about kale.

The Hardest Thing

Terry McGuire

My mom died in 2016, so it's too late to ask her why she'd wanted to hurt me that morning back in 1967.

Holding a cup of coffee in one hand and a glowing Kent in the other, she leaned her skinny backside against the Formica countertop in our kitchen and told me about a conversation that she and her lady friends had had during a dinner party the previous evening, after Lois McNulty asked, "If you were on a sinking ship with your husband and child and could save only one of them, who would it be?"

If she'd looked at me, she would have seen me holding my breath. But she didn't look at me; she took a drag off her cigarette and just stared into space. Until she finally exhaled and did look at me — straight in the eye, and said, "We all agreed; we'd save our husbands." I felt my body stiffen. But then she...sort of laughed, and for a brief moment I wondered if she was talking to me woman to woman. I mean, I'd gotten my period; I wore a bra. And, so, in that moment, I lightened, and I felt proudly grown-up.

Only then she went on, explaining, "We'd never be able to replace the guys, but we could always have another child." That said, she stubbed out the butt of her cigarette in an overflowing ashtray and walked away, leaving me there feeling small, alone, and terrified.

In high school, I enrolled in a Senior Life Saving class and became a certified lifeguard. It hadn't dawned on me then, but I wonder now, looking back, if it wasn't a cautionary tactic, a subconscious move "just in case." I'm relieved to say, years later, with two young daughters of my own, the training came in handy. My plan was that if we found ourselves on a sinking ship, I'd position the younger one on my back, secure my arm around the older one's chest, and swim sidestroke to shore; that way, I'd save all three of us. Later on, I enrolled my girls in swimming lessons to ensure that, with or without me, they'd always know how to stay afloat.

I'm not sure how or where I tucked away the pain brought on by my mother's cruel revelation, but in 1999 when my sister, my only sibling, died at the age of thirty-nine when I was forty-four, I assumed, based on my mother's short fuse with me, that she'd wished it was me who got cancer and died. To mourn the passing of beautiful, wonderful, gentle Lee — daughter, sister, wife, and mother of three — my mother self-medicated, drinking gallons of pink wine, which of course only made her that much meaner.

I had great difficulty comforting my mother after Lee's death. And I feared if I delved too deeply into the why of it, I'd actually drown. I nonetheless performed all the expected tasks of a doting daughter, hoping she'd eventually find some good in me, but I never seemed to get it right. She told me I was just so like Dot, the older sister she loved and hated, the aunt whom I adored.

My mother was agitated and confused on the day she died. At one point, I looked at her and said, "Mom, I don't know what you want from me." Then, in a moment of pure grace, I unclasped the necklace I was wearing, a crucifix, and I attached it around her neck, relinquishing my defeat to a higher power. And when I did, my mother looked up, bright-eyed and smiling. Before she died, my mother looked at me and smiled. Of course, I asked that she be buried wearing that magic necklace.

I've been married twice, proving husbands are replaceable. I never developed much of a knack for rescuing men, but what I do know with utmost certainty is that I'd sacrifice my life to save my daughters. Lucky for me, they both know how to swim.

 PROMPT: Write a piece that begins: *I don't know what you want from me.*

My Brother Yondre

Laura D. Roosevelt

The owner of the Green Acres cemetery in Columbus, Georgia, asked me how a fifty-five-year-old white Massachusetts woman came to be "closest of kin" to Yondre Davis, the eighty-seven-year-old Southern Black man whose plot I was purchasing. I explained that Yondre's mother, Nell, had raised me. My nanny since I was an infant, Nell worked for my family well past retirement age, in order to see me safely off to college.

Over the next twenty-two years, I came to know Nell out of her maid's uniform and in her house, not ours. I ate her food — collards with fatback, corn bread in a skillet. I learned she played the numbers daily, and when she won, we'd celebrate. I'd always known she snored, because hers was the bed I ran to as a child when frightened by thunderstorms; now I heard it from one room away.

Nell's home in Columbus was an hour's drive from the Georgia retreat that my grandfather, Franklin Roosevelt, frequented for polio treatments. Once, I took Nell, the granddaughter of slaves, to Warm Springs. I hadn't called in advance, but no need: The minute we got to the gate, Nell proudly announced to the attendant that here I was, her baby, a granddaughter of the president. We got the full tour, and Nell was aglow.

Our reunions always began and ended with the two of us embracing and sobbing — in joy when I arrived, in sorrow when I left. When I was growing up, Nell was the person who would always hug me, no matter what. I sometimes referred to her as my "second mother," but for Nell, there was nothing secondary about it; she called me "Baby" from the get-go, and now, when I visited, she'd put a maternal arm around me and proudly introduce me to her friends: "This here's my daughter, come all the way from Massachusetts to visit me." Her friends would nod approvingly and say, "Mm-mm-mm, that's a long way."

Yondre, Nell's son, lived with Nell until she died. I'd known him forever, but Nell's death in 1999 cemented our kinship. We two had adored this woman with a shared depth, and we held each other and cried when I stayed with him for her funeral. In her obituary, he named me as Nell's surviving daughter. We talked on Mother's Day and Nell's birthday that year, each making sure the other was holding up. Yondre, I could tell, wasn't. I worried that his sorrow was turning into depression. So as Thanksgiving neared, my family and I invited Yondre to come stay with us for the holiday. He did, and he did again every year afterward until his health began failing two years ago. Once he came for Christmas too, and twice the four of us visited him in Georgia. My children loved "Uncle Yondre," who spent hours on the floor with them, playing Candy Land and building Lego castles.

Last July, a friend of Yondre's called; Yondre had been found on his floor, confused and unable to stand. "You got to come take care of your brother," the woman said. I flew to Georgia. Yondre had suffered a stroke, and he also had vascular dementia. He was not going to get better, so I took charge — got power of attorney, found a good rehab/nursing home, brought necessities to Yondre from his house.

The house's condition told me that Yondre's dementia was not new. Yondre had always been fastidious about keeping his home pristine and his personal appearance "sharp." Now there were piles of papers everywhere, jars of creams in the bathroom missing their lids, and a mountain of unfolded laundry on the guest room bed. Yondre had always had a serious shoe fetish, organizing them by height and color on the floor of his closet, but now I found his shoes scattered and unpaired. Leaving the house, I sat in my car and wept.

Over time, as I made regular visits to Yondre in his nursing home, I got to know several of his friends, including Roy, a dapper retiree who had learned piano from Yondre as a kid. The last time

I saw Yondre alive, I met Roy at Ed's Country Cooking in nearby Phenix City, Alabama. Ed's was Yondre's favorite barbecue place, and I liked to pick up ribs, fried chicken, greens, and corn bread to take to him at the nursing home. This time, Roy and I got dinner for ourselves too, and we ate with Yondre, who was in good form that day. Leaving, Roy told me how happy he was to see how Yondre perked up when he saw me.

Roy and I have talked regularly since then, through Yondre's decline, final hospitalization, and death, and now in its aftermath. It might have been Roy who reminded me of Yondre's particular fondness for his red disco boots; I made sure Yondre was buried wearing them. At Yondre's funeral, Roy sat next to me, a comforting arm around my shoulders. People came to greet me and offer condolences to "Yondre's sister." It never ceased to amaze me that nobody in Nell's and Yondre's circle ever seemed to pay my whiteness any mind.

Recently, Roy asked whether he could call me his sister too. I said I'd be honored. "You know, Roy," I told him, "when Nell died, she left me Yondre. I loved him for keeping me connected to Nell, but also for himself. Now Yondre's died, and he's left me you."

Roy's reply reminded me of what I'd learned years ago when Nell left my parents' employ: Sometimes in endings, you find beginnings.

 PROMPT: Write a portrait of your nanny, literal or figurative.

The Hardest Thing

Taffy McCarthy

Dad died suddenly the night before he was to go into the hospital to lose weight. He left us alone in the new house that was supposed to make life easier. The new house...

My bedroom had new floral curtains, like a watercolor, with a matching bedspread. I had my own private bathroom, where I could scrutinize my evolving and unsatisfying face for hours. I would try out new lemon-scented potions with astringent properties to my heart's content. I was never going to be Cheryl Tiegs or Ali MacGraw no matter how much lotion or free time I had. That was for shit sure.

I had a walk-in closet with secret places for my teenage talismans, assorted memorabilia, and paraphernalia. Ticket stubs were tucked away in a shoebox with secret messages passed from girls I was newly friends with. Furtive missives, written on notebook paper with pink and purple mini-pens, were folded tightly into origami footballs and decorated with hearts, daisies, and balloon-y letters. These treasured notes were new evidence in my case for popularity, replacing my old fiction-filled diary that contained dubious stories, unreliable reporting, and outright lies (so that if anyone now or in the future ever read it, they shouldn't think I was such a total loser).

An orange antique typewriter ribbon tin, with a dark bonsai tree and a gold butterfly flying on it, contained two recently purchased doobies. And nothing could have screamed ILLEGAL POT STASH more clearly. If I had been on *Dragnet*, it would be the first place they'd look.

Maybe I was lucky that no one was paying that much attention; life was just rolling along. There was time to roam and think — or at least wander and wonder.

Then Dad died, Mom got sick, and reality crashed down. Like the skier wiping out in the opening credits of *Wide World of Sports*, I was falling at warp speed, somersaulting, ass over teakettle, gathering packed snow and debris, smashing and splintering through the icy guardrails into the endless void.

Some days my sister and I would get a memo from the school secretary: *Stay with the Nimocks — Mom is in the hospital again.* There was no advance warning so we could pack a toothbrush or a tampon or a *Peanuts* comic book or something.

I couldn't find any resting places or ways to catch up and get collected. I was disorganized, disconnected, and distracted to a fault. The days were like mercury: silver and slippy and amorphous.

I was lost 100 percent of the time. Some days, I went to school in the morning and found out in the afternoon that we were moving to the house of a different family.

And staying with other people with their freaky little foibles was exhausting. Everyone's house smelled weird — like Lavoris mouthwash and boiled meat. Trying to remember what deal-breaking rule went with which house was impossible. I usually discovered it five minutes after accidentally infracting it.

At the Sutras, the rule was: no double breakfasts. Either toast or cereal but not both. They watched me like a pot that never boils, almost daring me to exist in the kitchen space, sighing, grunting, raising an eyebrow at a loose jelly-jar lid, a drop of milk on the counter, crumbs in the...*Sorry, am I buttering too loud?*

The Webbs expected me to be ready for school and at the breakfast table at the ass crack of dawn. This was a problem because I could never find my knee socks and sometimes ended up wearing one blue and one green. And I didn't really eat breakfast.

This led to a contretemps with "Aunt Terry," who was all about breakfast. Even if I was late and not hungry (a little bit hungover and just wanting to get out in the fresh air for a smoke), I'd have to sit down and force-feed myself from all four food groups (a couple of slippery eggs, half a dozen rashers of bacon, a vat of oatmeal, fifty slices of toast, a gallon of OJ) in order to get the hell out of there and avoid a lecture on nutrition and punctuality, and the hairy eyeball from the freshly braided Betsy. *I wonder what the starving Biafrans are having this morning?*

Sleeping in became a thing of the past. Seriously. Just showing up seemed to be enough for everybody. As long as I let them know when I'd be back, and could account for every minute between now and my death, everything was hunky-dory.

I never knew what was going on. I just wanted to go live with Snoopy and Charlie Brown, where a cloud was a cloud, and dialogue and thought balloons were printed out in capital letters.

There was no letup and no outlet or letdown. I sleepwalked through the days on high alert. I knew it could all blow at any moment because it had, and it would again. Like when a deer jumps in front of the car out of nowhere while you're driving and you don't know if it's just the one or a whole herd. There was no reality check, no one to verify anything with. I'd suddenly remember things I needed and missed, or left at home, or hadn't seen for a while: my navy-blue cardigan, my softball glove, Mom.

Where was she? And when was I going to see her? Was she ever going to get dressed and go to PTA meetings or the A&P, or take me to get some new underwear? Were we ever going to go home and unpack? I didn't even know who was taking care of Ching or Susu.

Our friends and neighbors kept us alive on a C-ration of care, but I missed the boringness of afternoons at home, and chores I knew how to do, and the dull safety of parents to navigate the grown-up world and carry the weight of the everyday, so I could dream and doodle and form.

 ► **PROMPT:** The hardest thing

There's Silver in My Hair but Gold in My Heart

Nancy Slonim Aronie

Parenting and grandparenting are as different as farmers are from their ears of corn.

My grandmother reached just above my waist. It's true I am taller than most, but she was tiny. She had a perpetual twinkle, and when my sister and I would tease her (which for some odd reason we did often), she would laugh and her belly would do that thing you see in cartoons of jolly people. She was adorable. She tried to hide the fact that she was suffering from severe arthritis, but you could see it in the way she held her hands and rubbed her fingers. Her mantra, repeated constantly in Yiddish, was *hub nisht koi'ach* — "I have no strength." And she didn't. Not in her body, anyway. But her intuition was a powerhouse. Somehow she had known to gather my mother, age eleven, and my uncle, age seven, and convince her husband to leave Germany before the war.

My grandfather, also an adorable being, owned a small toy store in a poor immigrant section of Hartford, Connecticut. He got up at 6 every morning, carried the same lunch (rye bread slathered with about an inch of Land O Lakes butter) in wax paper, took two buses, and opened the shop promptly at 9 a.m.

As kids, my sister and I and our three cousins all worked in his store on Saturdays and after school. When I was twelve, a woman came in and asked, "Do you sell toboggans?" and my grandfather, without skipping a beat, said in his broken English, "Everytinks a bahggin." I remember being mortified. But when I was twenty-four, teaching high school in San Diego, he wrote me a letter with one long word: "venyougonagitmerit?" Translation: "When you gonna get married?" My embarrassment had by then melted into deep respect and extreme love.

Now it's my turn. I'm a grandparent, that magical role you hear will change your life. And it does. Finally it gives the hackneyed phrase *unconditional love* its actual meaning.

My husband and I just came back from Taos, New Mexico, where we took our thirteen-year-old grandson snowboarding. Why was it perfect? For one thing, we are not his parents. My friend Gerry jokes that the reason grandparents and grandkids get along so well is that they have a common enemy. Maybe that's true for some, but I think it's because as grandparents we don't have the *I'll love you if you play the flute. I'll love you if you go to Harvard. I'll love you if you're thin.* There's no *if.* There's simply *I'll love you.*

As a mom, I'm afraid I always had an agenda. I took my job seriously. And my job was to teach, to lead, to lecture, to guide, to decide, to pick, to choose, to control, to know everything.

I thought you could hand self-esteem to your kid like so many Legos in a tidy box, so when they showed me a drawing they had made, I acted with such hyperbolic fervor you would have thought they had discovered cold fusion in the pantry. It wasn't until they were already in college that I read Haim Ginott's book *Between Parent and Child,* explaining that it isn't your compliments they thrive on. It's your recognition of some detail. Look at the drawing, Ginott instructed, find something specific, and comment, as in: "Wow, that chimney looks just like the chimney at my best friend's house."

I remember wanting my older son to be on a swim team. He was a good swimmer but had no interest in swimming competitively. I drove him to swim meets. I found the best coach. I bought him the best goggles. I screamed in the bleachers. And I got the shelf ready for my...I mean his...I mean our Olympic gold medal. But it was my dream. Not his.

Our trip to New Mexico had all the ingredients of a travel nightmare. We were delayed by almost two days, stranded in the airport, then we had to sleep in the lobby of a hotel waiting for a room to open up. During the layover, we Ubered into the actual city of Baltimore, because the child said, "We're in Baltimore — we have to have crab cakes." (How does a thirteen-year-old know about Baltimore and crab cakes?) But of course we went, because we were taking our cues from our own family teen travel guide.

It turned out to be the absolute best trip ever.

But when we got home — exhausted, because traveling is

exhausting — I thought about all we had done physically and financially and psychologically.

And I said to my husband, "The last thing Gramma and Pappy would have done for me was schlep halfway across the country, spend their retirement savings on lift tickets, eat in a five-star restaurant (on no sleep), order the deluxe platter of crab cakes, king crab legs, shrimp, lobster, clams, mussels, and butter-soaked new red potatoes, and not be upset at the size of the leftover waste." No, they wouldn't have done any of those things. Not one.

But what they did do was let me be me. They didn't talk. They listened. They didn't judge, they watched. They weren't attached (as my teacher Ram Dass said) to the fruit of their actions. All they did was love me.

Now, because of what they modeled, I get the best gift a grandmother can get. Because who my boy is becoming is not coming from my need, and it isn't my job to make anything happen. I get the honor to watch, to listen, to not judge, and to support and see who my grandbaby actually is.

Take a trip with a grandchild. The journey is better than a year of therapy. And just about the same price.

 PROMPT: Write a short memory of your grandmother or grandfather. If you didn't have either, write about someone else's.

Introduce a Dramatic Scene

*I*f you want us to care about your story, there has to be drama. There has to be compelling action, something that engages us. Great words aren't enough. Great thoughts aren't enough. Great ideas aren't gonna keep us reading. What will keep us on the edge is your theater piece. What's next? What happened? Is everything gonna turn out OK? We have to worry and wonder. We have to have a relationship with the main character (you), hoping for an outcome, wondering if our hero (you) will make it. We must feel emotionally connected. And the drama is instrumental in accomplishing that. But dramatic doesn't have to mean serious. And funny dramatic stories can be just as engaging and endearing.

Tangier, 1969

Ellenora Cage

My mother carries a struggling baby goat in her arms, the heels of her purple suede go-go boots sinking into the mud as small children circle around her, taunting her, calling out, "Señora, señora!" She and her maid, Zorra, have walked out into the *Sharf*—meager strips of farmland just outside the city gates. My mother has decided to buy a baby goat, thinking it will be a good pet for us, only realizing her error after housing it on the rooftop terrace of our broken-down hotel, where it eats all her remaining underwear. After a few days, she gives the goat to the hashish dealer Mohammed as a present for *his* children.

We're all covered in sores. Except for my father, who has escaped the strange pox brought on by a virus, or malnutrition, or both. We're living in Tangier, Morocco, the White City, where my parents have come, according to my mother, "to write the great American novel." It is the second foreign country I have lived in, though I am not even two years old. Although I once had a photographic memory, I often wonder how much of Morocco I actually remember and how much I've put together from what I've been told. My mother tells me how six weeks after I was born, she and my father took me, my brother, a giant carton of Carnation instant milk, a box of Pampers, and my mother's tiny inheritance to make their way to Cuernavaca, Mexico. There they rented Malcolm Lowry's old house, where my father fantasizes that he'll write something akin to *Under the Volcano*. He emulates Lowry's raging alcoholism but fills his journals with more doodles than words except for the title on the cover — *Hot Nuts*, graphically collaged with a drawing of a cock and balls. My mother turns him on to Paul Bowles's novel *The Sheltering Sky*, and before the money runs out, they determine that Morocco is where the real Beats are making the scene and where my father will be able to find the artists who can dig and inspire his work. What better place to write the great American novel than in North Africa in 1969?

In truth, it's a pilgrimage to find the hashish, opium, and LSD that flood the seedy port city. They follow in the tracks of writers like Allen Ginsberg, William Burroughs, Jane and Paul Bowles, eventually meeting them in the decadent expat community camped out in the medina and the French Quarter. My father's charm, boyish good looks, and chutzpah will open many doors as he capitalizes on Bowles's and Burroughs's insatiable desire to surround themselves with young men.

My mother is taking more and more acid. She's come to

Morocco to find the music, the mysticism, and instead finds herself trapped in a hotel room with a screaming child in a country where women are sequestered in their homes like prisoners. Moroccan women only enjoy the sun and sky on their faces through the interior courtyards and rooftop terraces of windowless walled-up houses. "We like to keep our women out of view," Mohammed explains to my mother one day over a syrupy cup of mint tea. My mother is helpless to leave. As we are all on a family passport, she is tethered to her handsome, explosive husband, a mean drunk who disappears for days at a time. The days when he is gone, she finds some peace that shifts quickly to fear at his footfalls on the stairs and what sort of mood he might be in.

The Rolling Stones are in town. My father writes a note on the back of his birth certificate, saying he can score for them, and drops it at the front desk of their hotel. My mother is in love with Brian Jones and obsessed with Mick Jagger. She listens to their album *Aftermath* again and again, rocking her skinny body on the cotton-tufted floor mattress, covering herself with brightly colored wool Berber blankets, the hotel room's only source of heat. (My parents were sadly surprised to find the Moroccan winter cold and gray in contrast to the lush heat of Mexico.)

Mohammed picks up my dad with the necessary kif and hash to get them in with the Stones, intending to leave my mother and her sores behind. She is wrapped from head to toe in scarves to hide the angry blisters that have now covered her entirely, even erupting in her ears and nose. The woman my father is sleeping with has met the Stones in Ibiza and wants to go with Mohammed and him. They dump off her two kids with my mom. "Be cool," my dad warns her. "Don't mess up my scene," he says. Then as he trots down the stairs, he yells back at her, "You wouldn't want to go anyway with all those sores." Before they leave, my mother warily asks Mohammed how the goat is.

"He was good!" he says, smacking his lips.

They are off to find the Stones at a crumbling villa in the kasbah that belongs to Tatiana, a fake Russian countess, who is holding court.

My mother is at her end. Another long afternoon drags by as she stares down from the balcony. The white buildings are wrapped in cold gray haze; men's bodies, dressed in white djellabas, move freely in and out of the foggy openings in the street below. The two tabs of strong acid she's eaten are making her feel light again as she gazes over rooftops to the whitewashed medina in the distance. My five-year-old brother is at the public school learning Arabic and math, chanting the Koran. I am tottering around on the balcony, my diaper hanging low and wet as I watch my mother reach inside her red floral-print robe and remove her bra and falsies, laying the dingy fake breasts down on the cement. Distracted by their shape, I shuffle over to them as my mother perches on the stone wall of the balcony. She will tell me later that she was hearing Mick Jagger's voice calling out to her, floating through the airwaves past the white minarets. He sings, "I am waiting…I am waiting…" like a call to prayer for only her ears, penetrating the polluted sky. She will one day reassure me that she wasn't trying to kill herself, only going to meet God, chanting to herself, "If there is a God, then I am innocent. If there is no God, then I won't know." She reasoned that if she survived the fall, maimed or hurt, at least my father would leave her alone and quit calling her "poor little rich girl." But in that moment, long ago, I am wailing as she folds herself into a neat little ball and rolls off the balcony in front of me.

She falls three stories down through electrical wires that shock her but soften her fall as she breaks through them, landing in a dumpster full of glass Clorox bottles from the laundry below. Surprisingly, the fall leaves no visible marks on her body. Although her neck and shoulders will be chronically injured and she is broken inside, nothing else shows. The Moroccan ladies from the neighborhood rush out, their tattooed faces peeking out from under face scarves as they cluck softly in disapproval, while gently lifting her limp body from the garbage and hurrying her back inside the hotel. It is against the law in Morocco to commit suicide, and for a woman the penalty could be death. The irony of this is lost on the baby in a soggy diaper, screaming her head off, clutching a pair of rubber boobs still warm from her mother's body, wondering if she'll ever see her mother again.

My Take

The first time I heard this story was in my workshop at Kripalu in Stockbridge, Massachusetts. I was so blown away — and riveted by the drama — I couldn't even write down one word of feedback as she read it aloud.

With that opening sentence, how could you not want to keep going? You're caught immediately.

There wasn't a moment where I didn't believe this actually happened, but when Ellenora sent it to *Narrative*, a prestigious online magazine, she told me they loved it but asked if it was fiction. She adamantly said every word was accurate. She has absolute recollection of every detail, despite her young age. I believe her because I have heard this from other writers. So here we go.

"Purple suede go-go boots." And heels, no less. I've got the era, and I am getting a big hint as to who this woman is.

"Broken-down hotel." Big clue. What's coming?

The baby goat eating her underwear is funny, but how about the word "remaining"? In that one word we get the glimpse of a backstory. How long have they been there? Why is she out of underwear?

Hashish dealer. Uh-oh. What's going on? The setup using the words "present" and then "for *his* children" is brilliant, and of course we find out why later.

The line "we're all covered in sores" is chilling. Now there's a father in the picture, and why has he escaped the pox? And when she says "malnutrition," we are talking, in some circles, about child abuse. Neglect for sure. We are in the pocket of the narrator. Have been right from the beginning.

The cliché of writing the great American novel screams *loser*. And then she reveals that "it is the second foreign country I have lived in" even though "I am not even two years old." Now the reader is worried — this is a baby, for God's sake. And there are no adults around.

The line "Although I once had a photographic memory..." Ellenora put in because the editor of the magazine said it would be hard for a reader to believe. But when I heard it the first time, it didn't have that caveat and I believed it totally. However, I agree with the editor because you don't want the reader wondering instead of reading. And if you lose the attention of your reader to some detail that smacks of hyperbole or downright untruth, it will be difficult to get them back. So what she had to do works.

"He emulates Lowry's raging alcoholism but fills his journals with more doodles than words" just deepens our understanding of the mess these people are making of their lives. And we are thinking, *But it's not just their lives — they have these kids.*

"*Hot Nuts*" and then a graphic drawing. Oh no! Just oh no! It's perfectly placed here. We are already deeply committed to the narrator and trying to protect her. And this is just another example of the poor judgment of these parents.

The expressions "making the scene" and "dig" are right out of the Beat generation. It's authentic, and you can hear her parents talking now. The date 1969 is perfectly placed, just to clarify. We already know the era, but it's nice to have dates. Specific dates.

"My father's charm, boyish good looks..." is so cringeworthy. If we were worried before, the worry deepens.

Then, "my mother is taking more and more acid" makes you sit up and read it over. It's the kind of line that makes you go back and start reading the whole thing again. Because it's so packed.

"She's come to Morocco to find the music" and the words "trapped" and "sequestered" and "prisoners" are so visceral and visual. The alliteration of "*w*omen," "*w*indowless," and "*w*alled-up houses" is music. Then we cringe for an entirely different reason when Mohammed says, "We like to keep our women out of view."

The description of the father starts with "handsome," so you kind of expect the rest to be positive, but then come "explosive" and "mean drunk who disappears for days at a time." Up till now, we have nothing but contempt for this mother, but when we read the words "tethered" and "fear at his footfalls" (nice alliteration there), we are becoming a bit sympathetic to this overwhelmed mess of a woman. Then we hear she's "in love with Brian Jones and obsessed with Mick Jagger," and we're pissed at her again — it's her kids she's supposed to be obsessed and in love with!

Good detail of Berber blankets. Always details, please! Now we have the parents surprised by the cold and the gray, another indication of their total lack of maturity and vision. The line "intending to leave my mother and her sores behind" is pure power. "Angry blisters." OMG!!! Then she very casually throws in "the woman my father is sleeping with." "Be cool" (another expression from that era), "warns" (which is just so scary), "Don't mess up my scene," and "You wouldn't want to go anyway with all those sores," and we hate the father. The strong language, quotes, and images cause the reader to actually hate someone she has never met, will never meet, and who is only in someone else's story — this is a hallmark of great work. We are so emotionally invested and angry on this writer's behalf.

Then maybe the best line in the whole piece (not the writing of it but the meaning of it) is when the mother asks Mohammed how the goat is and he smacks his lips and says, "He was good!"

Could things get worse?

And they do. The paragraph from "My mother is at her end" to "rolls off the balcony in front of me" is so horrifying we can't breathe. "White buildings" and "white djellabas" is gorgeous.

The five-year-old brother is learning Arabic and chanting the Koran, while this two-year-old writer is taking in everything from the parents. The details of the "red floral-print robe" and the wet diaper and the "dingy fake breasts" are stunning.

Then "shape," "shuffle," "perches," and "stone" are music. Read your work out loud. I can't overemphasize how important it is for you to hear the *sound* of your words. But I'm willing to repeat myself ad nauseum. That's how important I think it is.

Mick Jagger singing, "I am waiting…I am waiting," "like a call to prayer." Yikes!!! Plus, "penetrating" and "polluted" — beautiful. The mother's drug-addled brain and her logic are the perfect recipe for disaster, which happens right in front of the writer. The "poor little rich girl" harkens back to the "tiny inher-itance" from the beginning. So if we aren't successful at trying not to be judgmental, right now we are thinking, *Poor little rich girl in-f**king-deed.*

The drama peaks with the vivid description of the fall and landing — electrical wires breaking her fall but shocking her, the dumpster of glass Clorox bottles, and the Moroccan ladies with "their tattooed faces peeking out from under face scarves as they cluck softly in disapproval." "Peeking" and "cluck" are perfect verbs. And of course "disapproval" and "garbage" speak volumes. "It is against the law in Morocco to commit suicide, and for a woman the penalty could be death" — oh my God.

And that last line, "wondering if she'll ever see her mother again" leaves your heart aching for the kid.

It's an absolutely perfect piece. I wish I had written it.

 PROMPT: Write an early, early memory.

The Shepherd Is My Lord

Tony Shalhoub

—For Mike. And David. And every dog gone.—

I've never thought of myself as a woo-woo kind of guy. With all candor, I would say I lean heavily, even boringly, toward the pragmatic. But for all that, I will admit, I have, on rare occasions, found myself more than a bit derailed by the "random" and inexplicable. The unsettling piece is that although the pragmatic is for the most part easy enough to retain, the random is utterly impossible to forget.

One such moment that rocked and rattled me occurred over a half century ago...but even now as I recount it, I feel my chest tighten and my stomach churn with queasiness.

On that rapidly darkening winter evening, there were six of us in the car, a massive clipper ship of a Buick (circa 1972) that belonged to my girlfriend's father. For no reason anyone can recall, I was driving. Across from me, curled up in the passenger seat, was my best friend, Micker, snoozing his way to comatose. Behind us, in the comically spacious back seat, was flopped Micker's girlfriend, Nancy, leaning gently on her best friend, who was my girlfriend, also named Nancy (I know, right?!), and lastly, my Nancy's older brother, David, half straddling, half hugging his somewhat less than car-friendly-sized German shepherd, Adolf. (I know, right?)

We were on our way home from a long-weekend ski trip, having stayed at my Nancy's family's rustic, romantic lakeside cabin, not far from the mountain but nearly three hours' drive from our hometown.

The past three days had been gloriously exhausting! We'd skied our buns off (as we liked to say) and stayed up late every night talking, laughing, eating, making out, and recklessly draining unwholesome and unhealthy quantities of the least-expensive wine and beer available to high school seniors in the early '70s. (For the record, the drinking age in the state at the time was eighteen, so possibly three of us qualified.)

The long car ride was mostly uneventful. There wasn't much traffic, and the two-lane roads were nearly dry. This handsome automobile wasn't new to me; I'd been allowed to drive it once or twice before, and I was always struck by how beautifully it handled. Damn, it was comfy!

A little too comfy?

After a couple hours, the sporadic bursts of conversation from the rear seat slowly dwindled, and I became aware that the two Nancys had completely checked out. Mercifully, David would intermittently toss a question up to me or attempt to draw Adolf's gaze to a mysterious mound of roadkill caught in the high beams. No doubt David was trying to ensure I was staying alert. And I was…I was…I really was…that is, until at one point he sort of paused midsentence and did not resume. The quiet of that disquieting pause gradually morphed into faint snoring…and I realized that from here on out it was just me — and the roadkill.

Before long, I found myself tightly scrunching my eyes shut — for just a second or two — to clear my blurring vision, as my eyelids were now on an involuntary yet relentless expedition south.

Looking back, I sometimes ask myself why I didn't simply pull over, either to rest or to ask one of the others to take the wheel. But I always come up empty. I honestly don't remember.

What I *do* remember, or rather the next thing I remember, is the feeling of a gentle but persistent nudge on my upper arm, just below the right shoulder, with just enough force to rock me slightly and…wake me up? Only one bleary eye opened, but the headlights revealed we were approaching — at 48 mph! — nothing but trees…and a ninety-degree bend in the road ahead. Before I could even think to take my foot off the gas, I cranked the wheel to the right and, with the two left tires hugging the shoulder, sailed through the turn.

It was the dog. It was Adolf. His paws were on my seat back, and his formidable snout was now resting smugly against my arm.

Perhaps it's a testament to the smoothness of that Buick's suspension, or perhaps it was the three and a half days of teenage debauchery, but despite the abruptness of my white-knuckle swerve, none of my sleeping passengers stirred. Of course, my adrenaline was now raging to maximum rpm's, so I saw no point in spoiling their slumber or recruiting a new driver. And full disclosure: I wasn't ready to "share" my experience (or reveal my stupidity). That would have to wait for at least a month or two.

Prior to this adventure, I hadn't had strong feelings about David's dog one way or the other. He had been trained, I guessed, to be a "one-person" pet. And, like David, Adolf was a bit...unpredictable. Somewhat tightly wound. (Did I mention that his name was Adolf?) OK, truth be told, I was afraid of him! We all were. But after this strange, unbelievable, random, inexplicable *lifesaving* gesture, my fear transformed into worship. And love. And gratitude.

And how's that for woo-woo?

 PROMPT: Write about an "almost" in the car.

The Hardest Thing

Daphne Freise

The cold dampness is unpleasant but not uncomfortable enough to motivate me to leave our unfinished basement. Not enough to make me peel myself from the floor where I lie prone. Certainly not enough to compel me to face the fourteen stairs leading to a hallway filled with framed watercolors I brought home from Venice and scenes from Varanasi, where the Ganges River flowed with cremated remains of souls seeking their next vessel.

The top step demarcates the basement, where I come for solitude. Where I wallowed in angry grief over my father's slow murder and wrote his obituary excluding my stepmother, his widow, and the heavy-metal poisoning that screamed in hair roots plucked from his body.

It's where I come to get grounded after a workweek on the private jets of the rich and famous. I come here to quiet the tormenting memories of the senior captain who locked his arms around my arthritic neck, squeezing and flexing as he shouted vulgar desires, what he likes to do to "boys," his beer-soaked spittle landing on my face and hair. Here is where I wrestle with fury that he was a known serial predator for two decades. That he violated and threatened at least a dozen other flight attendants, exposing himself, breaking into their hotel rooms, frightening them awake the moment he crawled into their beds after undressing. That a mind like that was still at the flight controls of some of the most powerful, discriminating people on earth.

The rest of the house is where I pretend to be doing all right. But down here, among Rubbermaid tubs filled with holiday decorations and shelves of tools, hardware, and paint cans, I'm breathing the least healthy air in the house. Still, I don't want to leave where I lie on a bright-orange rug.

This is my boho-hippie space, my Bedouin-style tent fashioned from wall-sized fabric panels. Colorful tie-dye swirls have been painted onto a black cotton background, and silhouette elephants march in a circular mandala.

It wasn't the most rational thing to do, constructing a cotton tent in this dank environment. But once two gut-wrenching crimes struck within a six-week span, I didn't have the bandwidth to think rationally.

I crave a break from my constant, racing thoughts. Lying belly down on the basement floor brings me closer to calm. For some odd reason, as I melt into the one last layer that lies between me and the earth, quiet comes.

My head is turned to offset straining my scoliotic neck, and my left eyelashes brush the carpet. I take another shallow breath and focus on the edge that has begun to unravel from kitty scratches. Just beyond the straggly fibers is exposed concrete. Red paint chips and peels. Granules of gray litter have dropped off Copper and Sophie's paws and freckle the floor, evidence of nocturnal investigations around my special place. A musty stench clashes against scented carpet freshener.

I don't want to see, think, or feel. I want all the clawing thoughts to get their talons out of my head, but when I close my eyes, I become dizzy. When I keep them open, it feels like someone is dragging sandpaper against them.

I hear the garage door motor. My patient, worried husband is home from his bike ride and will be looking for me, his heart and brain freshly saturated with happy oxygen — exactly the opposite of mine. The ice dispenser rattles to cool a glass of Gatorade. Dripping sweat and out of breath, he will relate squirrel near misses and how a negligent driver nearly hit him. I should get up before he sees me like this.

Now he's going upstairs to the bedroom to get out of his wet clothes. I need to get up, but if he gets into the shower before searching the house for me, I can have a few more minutes on the floor with rotting paint and cat toys.

The swishing of water rushes through the drainpipes now. He is rinsing off the ride, and it is time for me to tie up my thoughts and pry myself up. He deserves more of me, better of me.

He doesn't even know about the darkest places I've gone since finding out about Dad's poisoning and, just five weeks later, the violent assault at work.

The shower noise stops. I shake out of my mind a disturbing image that has begun to visit me with increasing frequency. Train tracks. Anna Karenina.

Lifting my feet to clear each step, I meet Tim at the top stair with a kiss and a smile. He thinks this is one of my good days. Lying to him should be the hardest thing, but letting him see the truth would be so much harder.

 PROMPT: Write about your refuge, and describe in detail where you go for solitude. If this doesn't resonate, interview three friends, ask if they have places they go to be alone, and write the detailed descriptions. And write how you feel not having a special place.

I Should Have Known...

Julia Kidd

When the first messages came through, on Facebook, in private, it had been twenty-three years since we'd spoken. He had a reputation then. Had even flirted with me while dating my roommate. But still, people change, don't they?

The first few messages were innocent enough. Something about a longtime crush.

Then so sympathetic about my dead dog. There could have been no softer spot for entry.

He remembered the way I blushed during a critique of my work as an eighteen-year-old art student showing my raw and angry paintings for the first time.

He was barely thirty himself yet seemed so much older and wiser at the time. A hot New York artist, SOHO and all that. Those things mattered then, but now the gap had narrowed. The age difference seemed insignificant. No longer in need of connections, I had given up art making long ago and was set with a house and a healthy career of my own.

"I can't get enough of you," he wrote.

And so it was. The wick was thin. Once lit, fire traveled fast. Our communication was lyrical and sweet and playful. "The poetry between us," he called it. Several times a day back and forth, sharing music we listened to, art we liked, and pictures we took. I made videos with my phone documenting my world: Illumination Night lanterns, a clothesline with snapping sheets, holiday lights blinking in the mist. Trite, I know, but all excusable when bitten by love.

We shared the details of our lives.

"I made carrot soup."

"My mother used to make carrot soup."

"I went to the film festival."

"Tell me everything you saw."

"The key sticks. I think I need a locksmith."

"Just put some graphite in the keyhole," he offered.

Not exactly a boyfriend but handy just the same. I bought new underwear. Twenty pounds disappeared.

"I'm behind you. I have my arm around you. I'm kissing your back."

Between my legs was a juicy ache. I was operating with magic beans in my pocket. He sent me pictures of himself.

"This is what I look like now."

I already knew. Of course, I had googled, found a few articles, reviews of his work, and there were photos, mostly with students, their arms around their beloved teacher. I studied each carefully, the clothing, his shape, and the gesture of his hands.

But the kind of pictures that came later, were, well…not found on Google.

OK.

We are adults. It seemed a natural progression. And in return I took some pictures of my own, nothing too trashy. My rule was to never send him anything I would be sorry if other people saw.

In the beginning I used my camera and the timer, but later I just took selfies. Lighting helped, and just so you know, posing on your back makes your stomach look flat. I kind of got into it. Think, artistic.

One evening, when my phone seemed to slow down, I did what anyone would do and asked the nearest teenager. My son and his friend Mikey moaned and teased me about my technical incompetence like kids do.

"Let me see it," offered Mikey, the more willing of the two.

"Thank you," I said, putting dishes in the sink.

"Mom, I told you, you need to download your data," my son said as they went upstairs to plug into the desktop. I took out the trash, then the compost. I was wiping the counter when the first duet of cries reached my ears.

"Oh my God! Holy shit."

And I knew — believe me, I somehow Jesus-H-Mary-and-Joseph just *knew* — in that speed-of-sound instant, there was no way to stop it. I moved toward the stairs just as the next verse of "OH MY GOD" was delivered. A little bit louder and a little bit worse, as the old song goes. The voices of boys turned half men at this point. I flushed hot in the face. My stomach collapsed with some bottomed-out stab of regret.

You know how it works, the download, how the photos fly by as they make their way from smartphone to computer? Miraculous really. They flip by like a movie. Only in this case, it's kind of a dirty movie, starring your mother.

And those photos I sent? The ones I promised I wouldn't be upset if other people saw?

Well, they were now full-screen viewing for my seventeen-year-old son and his friend.

"What is that? An apple?" questions Mikey who squints closer to the screen when the one where I'd placed a Dahlia between my legs flashes past.

And Dear Lord.

My poor boy, his eyes shielded by hands, continued his new trauma mantra, "Oh my God. Oh my GOD."

He backed away, until he was just under the pull string that releases the stairs to our attic. Reaching up, he gave it a tug and began to climb, his feet slow and heavy, a sound like a moan (or was it a wail?) coming from his throat.

"Years of therapy might undo this one," he said when he reached the top, vanishing into the dark other region of our once-peaceful home.

"Well, now you know..." my panicked justification began, "your mom has a sex life...sort of..."

I spoke as quickly as I could into the total nonlistening void, "You know about war and the slaughter of animals, and now you know a little bit more about relationships..."

Louder now, but mostly to myself. "Love between people is a beautiful thing. There is no shame in this."

At some point he came down from the attic, and somehow my phone was unplugged and handed back to its slutty owner. We never mentioned it again, but Mikey hung around a lot more after that. I was a wreck, but once the house quieted down, who do you think I called?

 PROMPT: Write a story about a time you were totally embarrassed.

A Freak Storm

Bradford Rowe

Here it is the end of April, almost May Day, nearly the halfway point between the spring equinox and the summer solstice, and it's snowing to beat hell outside tonight.

About nine thirty, the nurse and a screw (aka a guard) go running by on the way to Segregation. This is not out of the ordinary, and since my cell is on "main street," I've gotten used to it. But then a guard goes by, then another, then the night captain. Something's up.

I can hear the questions coming from the other cells down the corridor. "Hey, did you see who that was? Looked like the night captain." "Must be some action up in Seg — maybe somebody had a heart attack or something." About twenty minutes go by with nobody coming back through. Then in the night-light gloom I see the warden stroll by with yet another screw.

The last time I saw him after our nightly lockdown was the time they took P off my corridor for attempted planning to escape. There I was, watching the tube, when I look up and see P looking back at me out on the runway. When the cell door opens after lockdown there's only one reason: Somebody's going for a ride, and you're just glad it's not your door that opens.

Trying to get information from the screw or the night nurse is no good. A little later a suit goes by, and I can see he's a state detective, followed later by an old medical examiner and a screw carrying the examiner's bag. He tilts his head as he goes by, asking, "Where is it, up in Seg? Yeah, that's where it usually happens."

Warden walking back toward center block, and I hear somebody from down the corridor, "Hey Mr. Magnusson, what happened up in Seg?" He stops a second, then turns to the bars, hands still in his pockets, and answers, "Somebody hung up in Seg." Later

I learn it was the new guy, just in, that killed himself. He only had a couple of years to do and freaked out because of the false horror stories they'd told him down in County. Here, he was in Seg under suicide watch. And they don't watch.

This type of death no longer shocks me since the crash course in self-destruction I got in the county jail just waiting for trial. Three guys cut up, one three times before they dismissed his case. One tried to burn or choke himself on the smoke but chickened out at the last minute. One tried to hang himself twice, and he almost made it the second time. We were all in the day room playing cards, and he tied up in the cell not five feet from where I was sitting watching him turn red to blue. The screw coming around on the regular check looks in the cell, then takes a step, does a double take, and runs in to cut the guy down. We just kept playing cards while they revived him enough to drag him out. These were all people not even sentenced yet. That was when I figured out that the screws weren't there primarily to keep you from escaping but to keep people alive long enough to stand trial. Once you're found guilty and sentenced, you're wards of the state and can be punished for trying to destroy state property.

The coroner has gone by and the body bag been rolled out. It's still snowing, but it will probably be gone by tomorrow afternoon or the next day. The cell in Seg will have a new occupant by tomorrow night. I wonder how the news will play this up tomorrow. Mostly they do the old prison horror story routine, when it's just some kid alone and scared checking out in Seg. It will give the boys something to talk about for a couple of days and then be forgotten like the freak snow we got tonight.

 PROMPT: Write about a freak storm.

Let It Break

Joy Reichart

A few years ago I was in a state of, shall we say, spiritual disorientation. A limbo between a very solid What Had Been and a blackly obscured and unknowable What Was to Be. That liminal state where it feels like there's no ground under one's feet (usually because, in every respect but the physical, there isn't). All I knew for sure was that everything felt wrong. All I felt able to do was wander around — literally. Searching, maybe, or simply keeping moving lest I get sucked into the black hole that yawned, terrifyingly, at the edge of my consciousness.

In retrospect, I was in the very early stages of one of the most massive, devastating, and necessary changes of my life. This feeling was life shaking me awake from what had become a deep and complacent slumber — *You are more than this*, it whispered. *Time to move on; time to get going; what lies ahead you have no way of knowing*, it irksomely quoted Tom Petty.

I had no conscious inkling of this at the time, though. I just felt generally unsettled and awful, with nothing I could point to as a reason. There was no evident injustice causing my despair, no major loss inspiring this grief. It was coming purely from within — utterly invisible and impossible to describe, so I didn't try. I didn't tell anyone. Instead, I wandered through the hills near my home, crying a lot, not understanding. I wasn't suicidal but had the thought more than once that if death came for me, I wouldn't mind. I'd go quietly.

It was rough.

One day my wanderings took me to a familiar hiking trail, drew me toward a familiar tree. It wasn't a particularly magnificent specimen, just a scraggly old pine whose lowermost foot of grayish bark had fallen or been scraped off. It seemed elderly. It was a being that I always felt compelled to greet in some way, with a touch or a wave, as I moseyed by.

That day I stopped, my heart full of questions that had no words. I leaned against my tree, back to trunk, breathed, breathed, my inner critic judging me as usual for being pathetic and dramatic. My ego terrified of being seen by anyone who passed by.

Despite all this, as soon as I connected to the tree, I felt the web of intelligence it shared with all the other trees, with the ground, the ancestors beneath, the sky above, the All of It. The whisper of breeze through the leaves overhead, the rustling of life in the undergrowth — none of it was random noise. It was the harmonious hum of all existence, the lucid voice of the Everything.

I was in a holy place, I knew. Guidance was available. I didn't know what to say. What to ask. I just knew I needed help. So, I asked for that. Asked for help.

Listened. Nothing.

I feel like my heart is breaking, came my silent confession.

Then let it break, I heard in noiseless response.

I did. Then and there, the elderly tree still holding me, I let my heart break. A quiet, heaving, knowing sob. An opening, finally, into the expanding territory of my soul. A painful stretching to take in all I was becoming aware of. Permission, finally, to feel it all — even the stuff that hurt. Especially the stuff that hurt. It swept in to fill me for a moment. It was nearly more than I could bear, but enough to glimpse where this all was going.

Ever so briefly, just then, I felt my place in the world again. The tree helped me see not only where the ground was, but where my ground was. For an infinitesimal moment, I could almost make out where I was headed. It was a place I didn't understand yet. There were no answers, but there was information.

Let it break. My heart needed to break, to crack open to allow for this expansion. Much of my suffering had come, I realized, from trying to keep it together, when clearly "it" was not even a thing anymore. I'd been holding fast to a flimsy branch as the current of life endeavored to move me downstream.

There was also the suffering caused by trying to leave the darkness too soon. An old metaphor that never fails to wow me is that of caterpillars transitioning into butterflydom. They literally liquefy in their chrysalis. This cannot be comfortable. Interview any moth you meet, and they will not, I'm sure, look back upon their cocoon days with nostalgia and longing.

And it doesn't end there: They must, once they awaken — with giant new wings wound around them in this space that is suddenly too small and stifling — fight their own way out, however long it takes. To help a butterfly out of its cocoon is to kill it. It must break out on its own.

So must our souls, stirring in the confines of what is no longer ours to be. There has to be a break, a tear, a rending, as we emerge new into the blinding light. None of it is comfortable. All of it is necessary. It is nature. Our nature.

It took ages, lots more miles of hiking and plenty more pain, but eventually my outer world did come into alignment with what I was catching foggy glimpses of in those first days. I eventually made my way out of the chrysalis, tottered confusedly for a bit in the blinding newness, and grew accustomed to the new self that had been gestating during all those months of perplexity and pain.

It's the hardest work of our lives, to recognize something is amiss, acknowledge that where we are is no longer relevant and that something else is calling to us. To not deny it, fix it, contain it, or even define it. And definitely to not paint a veneer on it so that things still seem shiny and OK. On the contrary, we need to move forward into the mystery. To allow our hearts and our worlds to break, to be upended, to sit in the dark and let ourselves liquefy. Trusting that eventually we will emerge and unfold into something far bigger than our old minds can just now hold.

► **PROMPT:** Write about a break, a tear, a rending you experienced and where it took you.

Mission: Possible

Nancy Slonim Aronie

At the height of the women's movement and at the very beginning of our pot smoking days we were invited to a party with people we mostly didn't know.

My infant son Dan had just been diagnosed with juvenile diabetes, and I was tired, dark circles under my eyes and an extra thirty pounds on my hips, and if you cared to look closely you could see in my face that I had a baby who wished he had a different mother, one who wasn't sticking needles into his teeny thighs and then a split second later trying to comfort him.

I think I tried on about nine outfits before I finally settled on something that I thought could hide my metaphorical weight as well as the actual poundage.

We were barely over the threshold when a sexy young blonde ran up to Joel, grabbed his hand, and pulled him onto the dance floor. He didn't resist.

You know how there are certain types of women you are so not but wish you were? She was mine. She had that dancer's body, with her feet pointed out and that ballet dancer walk (which I have tried to imitate to no avail). Her hair was what I was paying top dollar with blow-dryers and big rollers to emulate. She was about five-two, and since that was my height at birth, that cute diminutive look had been in my rearview mirror for decades. I must have been invisible because they both went off as if I weren't even there.

I watched them dance and thought, *Of course he'll leave me for her. I am fat. I am ugly, and I'm not even a good mother. I can't make my baby stop crying. I broke his pancreas because I smoked pot. I'm irresponsible and unreliable and undependable. And if my baby dies it will be my punishment for being a BAD MOTHER!* The loop began again: *I'm unattractive, obese, and no fun…*

I made my way to the food table. There was a big cooked ham in the center. I remember removing the clove, then the maraschino cherry, and then the pineapple ring from the top of the whole ham and glaring at Joel, who must have felt the laser-focused dagger energy. I sliced off a square of fat and said in my head, *You think I'm fat now? Wait, asshole. I'll show you fat!* I ate as if I were about to run a marathon. Carbed up, chowed down.

I was down the rabbit hole of self-defeating thoughts, and until hours later, I remained at the bottom, with Joel nowhere to be found (not that I was actively looking). When he did emerge, rumpled and contrite, I glared at him and out we walked. I put on a fake smile for the hostess, who I was sure couldn't wait to call her girlfriends and say, "You know that Nancy Aronie? She looks like a cow, and her husband is fooling around. And *who* is still wearing midi skirts?!?"

At this point in my head, I had pretty much gotten divorced and was an obese single mom with two kids, one of whom was sick, and no income.

The minute we got into the car and before Joel put the key in the ignition I started pummeling him. I had never hit anyone in my life. I was so out of control I actually missed and banged my wrists on the headrest. He deflected my blows, protesting all the while — *"Nothing happened. Jesus, Nance, nothing happened!"*

I said, "I don't care if nothing happened. I don't care if you two solved the f**king unified field theory while nothing happened. I did not need to be sitting there humiliated with people I don't even know!"

We drove home in silence. We pulled into the driveway and sat there. My mother was sleeping over, so we didn't have to rush a babysitter home.

Finally I said, "If you want to f**k around, go f**k around. But don't ever, ever, ever do that to me again!"

"I didn't do anything," he protested. "It's just that there's this huge party going on, and I can't go because society —"

"Oh please! Society!" I snapped.

"Women are crawling all over the place, and I am not allowed to even —"

"Oh, poor Joel," I whined. "He's married to a loser, and now he's stuck and can't have any fun. It must be just horrible for you."

"It's not horrible," he said, "but don't you look at other guys sometimes?"

"No!" I barked. "I don't look at other guys any time. It took me most of my life to find the one I wanted. Through sickness and through health, in case you have forgotten."

He took that in and countered with, "Everyone is f**king around, and you want to just stay home and sit on the couch watching *Mission: Impossible.*"

"Yes, as a matter of fact that's exactly what I want to do!" I screamed.

"I feel like I'm missing something revolutionary culturally and I'm on the outside looking in. Why can't we just experiment and see how it goes?"

"See how it goes?" I screamed louder. "SEE HOW IT GOES???!!!! I'll tell you how it's gonna go. Some little blonde dancer, just like the one tonight, who doesn't walk around exhausted with dark circles under her eyes with bad breath because there's no TIME to gargle with Listerine, who hasn't neglected to change her bra in three weeks because her boobs hurt too much, is gonna waltz into your life, and she's gonna smell good and laugh at all your stupid jokes and dance and be thin and have perfect hair, and you're gonna waltz right outta here. And I wouldn't exactly blame you either. If I could leave me, I'd leave me too."

My husband has always been slower in fights than me. He is

not quick with an angry quip. He's not even slow with an angry quip. He doesn't have a sarcastic or angry bone in his body, and he's not mean. And at this point, he was just young. Not chronologically but emotionally. And the timing of the women's movement couldn't have been worse for my marriage.

We were both exhausted. We were constantly worried about money. Our sex life, which had never been Marlon Brando and Eva Marie Saint, had devolved to "Maybe tomorrow I'll have feeling in my body again, honey."

He looked shocked and hurt. "Nance," he said, "what are you talking about? I'm not looking for a wife! I'm not looking to go anywhere. I just want to have what everyone else is having right now. A little extracurricular activity."

He forgot to say, "You're not fat, you're beautiful," and, "I already have the best wife in the world." Instead he said, "Can we keep discussing this?"

My mother found us sitting at the kitchen table still talking at daybreak. It was Sunday. The last thing we said to each other was "No matter what we decide, we must remember to be kind and careful with each other."

I was punch-drunk from no sleep and a broken heart when the phone rang later that day. It was my former student who had been our marijuana connection.

"I'm going to London tomorrow," she said. "Your new dealer's name is Bob. I gave him your phone number."

The next morning, just after I had put the kids down for their naps, the phone did indeed ring.

Weary and semiconscious, I said a half-hearted hello. And something in the way he sounded woke me up from a long winter's asexual nap. I'll never know if it was that I was so wounded from the harsh rejection of the night of the party or whether he really had an unusually sexy voice, but for some reason, before he arrived for what he called our "business meeting," I applied my kohl black eyeliner more mindfully than usual and put on a T-shirt that had my nipples singing, "There's no business like show business."

I didn't yet know a phrase like "the universe sent him to me" but if I had, that's what I would have been thinking. However, there was no thinking. There was only a feeling I had never felt before. I was vibrating. My body was shaking. And I knew only one thing: I had to be with this man. Within twenty minutes, we were in the attic on the mattress Joel had thrown up there in case we ever had guests who were too tired to drive home.

There was no more weariness that morning, but there was definitely a driving home.

When Bob left, I tried to process what had happened. I sat and stared at the leaded-glass eyebrow windows that were letting in the pink morning light. I waited for my heart to stop pounding.

I floated around for the rest of the day probably more loving to the world than I had ever been. Couldn't stop smiling or looking at myself in the mirror.

And when Joel walked in from work, I didn't skip a beat before I blurted, "So I did it with the drug guy today."

He smiled and said, "So how was that?" I said, "It was fine." My breathing had just returned to normal, so I sounded normal.

"So now do you see what I mean?" he said.

I think I thought he was going to say, "Where is he? I'll beat the crap out of him." In fact, that's what I'd wanted. And then we could go back to being us. Imperfect but us. Not only would beating the crap out of someone be completely not Joel's nature, but that is not at all how he felt. He was triumphant like he had gotten his point across. And me? Well, I was devastated. I thought the definition of love was ownership, possession, jealousy, so he must not really love me.

It turned out Bob was the perfect antidote to my wounded

heart. I saw the wounded poet. A poster of James Dean had hung on my teenage bedroom wall, and now here was his doppelgänger right in my actual house. He was twenty-four. I was thirty-two. He was a born lover. I was new at anything to do with my body. And he had everything to do with it.

But now I had to justify my change of heart about opening up the marriage. My rationale was that we had practically been virgins when we got married. No one could have premarital sex. Abortion was illegal. And the birds-and-bees lecture I had gotten at home was "Your only currency is your reputation. If it's soiled, no one will want you — no one decent anyway."

So Joel was right. We had been missing a party. But I was right too. It was scary as anything.

We sat down and wrote a list of sensible rules:

Always tell the truth.
No betrayal. No deceptions.
No married people.
No people in our social circle.
No playing tennis or having blueberry pancakes with her/
    him in the morning.
No one sleeps in our bed. (I don't think we stuck to that
    one.)

And so we got to have a high school redo where instead of being terrified and insecure about our raging hormones, we were thirty-two-year-old teenagers, still raging but with a bit of grown-up consciousness.

 PROMPT: Write about a relationship challenge and how you resolved it.

Discover and Reveal
a New Insight about Yourself

*I*t's your *one-of-a-kind* perspective that makes your essay relevant. As a reader, I don't just want to be entertained. I want to learn, to grow, to find another way of seeing, another way of being. I am looking for a map. When you share your insights, you share an intimacy that says more about you than any factual information. It says, *This is who I am. This is what's important to me*, and then I have the choice as to whether I make some changes in my own way of seeing or take some time to consider yours and maybe discard it completely or cherry-pick what I liked. Giving us your real take on things, and letting us see you evolve through the course of the essay, makes the narrative much deeper and more meaningful and demonstrates your ability to think critically.

Sorry Your Brain Broke. Here's a Casserole.

Judith Hannah Weiss

In my first life, I parked one word next to the other, and they stayed where I put them. This was called "freelance writing," and it meant morphing my voice so *Wired* would sound, well, like *Wired*, Elmo would sound like Elmo, *Elle* would sound like *Elle*, and *Rolling Stone* would sound a bit stoned.

I knew where to start, how to end, and where to go in between. It wasn't all the news. Just the hits, the misses, the hissy fits, the highs, the lows, the pits. The hip little shake, the little hip shake, plus what raises hemlines, what raises heart rates, what raises hell.

The first company I worked for owned time and life and people. I mean *Time* and *Life* and *People* plus *Money* and *Fortune* and Martha Stewart and CNN and HBO. It was called Time Life. I began on staff, then became a freelancer, and later, a part-time ghost. My clients owned Oprah and Martha and *Vanity Fair*, plus *Vogue*, *The New Yorker*, and Kermit the Frog.

I spent decades telling folks how to prevent everything bad, protect everything important, and procure everything good. All they wanted or needed to know, have, want, wear, buy, try, lose, use, taste, sip, skip, slip into or out of.

Then, at 10 a.m. on a Tuesday, a drunk driver stole a truck and compressed a parked car. I was in the car.

My name is J. I used to have a name with more letters, but that was before the truck. They test my head hundreds of times and find lots of things have disappeared. Like the file that encodes new memories and the file that integrates physical movements so you don't fall out of your chair. Aphasia gouged words. Amnesia gouged most everything else.

It was the same type of injury former congresswoman Gabby Giffords suffered when she was shot in the head. I point to a chair because I can't say "chair." I do the same with a shoe. I mime drinking from a bottle because I can't say "bottle" or "water" or "drink."

1

I couldn't say "shower."
I couldn't say "cup."
I couldn't say "down."
I couldn't say "up."
I couldn't say "please help me put on my socks."
A repurposed object is something that acquires amnesia and

forgets what it did before. A "repurposed" human reconfigures any shards she can find of anything she ever knew, like she always just missed a step or a train or a decade. There are a few more problems too. Like the phone weighs two hundred pounds. So does my right hand. My left hand weighs slightly less. My feet weigh slightly more.

I have "more or less aphasia" combined with "more or less amnesia" at any given time. There is no conversation, and no one comes over to say, "We're sorry your brain broke, so here's a casserole."

I imagine my brain as a jigsaw puzzle of the United States. Kansas drops out. Then the entire Northwest is gone. Kansas reappears, but there's no mid-Atlantic. San Diego disappears along with Chicago and Santa Fe. Chicago reappears. Things blow up. They didn't come with a warranty. Neither did I. What didn't blow up seems to break down. That is called getting old.

This is not a drill. Someone in scrubs puts more of something in the IV. Perhaps it is anti-aging, anti-wrinkle, anti-old. Perhaps it sucks out cellulite. Perhaps it just sucks. Some days go better than others. Some people are from another planet. Perhaps I am one of them. I was a professional. I imagined things. Then something no one could imagine happened. Someone ran out of beer and crushed a car that contained me.

The brain controls muscles and everything else. Muscles are fueled by mighty chondria, I mean mitochondria, which convert food to energy and make you gorgeous, sexy, strong. The more of them you have, the more gorgeous, sexy, and strong you are. Or not.

2

My legs twitched and my feet were forever falling asleep. My left eyelid drooped. My smile was crooked. My right hand hurt like hell. So did my head. Each word was a language problem. Each step was a math problem. The odds of a sinkhole opening within me were approximately equal to the odds that I'd find the right word at the right time. Or — even more important — the odds I could build a bridge to my child.

Aphasia is caused by damage to areas of the brain where language is held. Where language "is held" sounds beautiful. Where language "was held" does not. Words jammed in my ears if I heard them. Jammed in my throat if I tried to say them. Jammed in my head if I saw them. This is called not making sense.

Things I couldn't say reminded me of other things I couldn't say. But somehow there remained a spark of me in me that I fanned into flame because no one else could. I began scratching anything I could recall onto any surface I could find — paper plates, paper cups, place mats, napkins, coffee stirrers, and Popsicle sticks. I called them scraps. They were not in alphabetical order, not in numerical order, not in chronological order, but out of order, like me.

A doctor arrived. She said something about not wanting to pressure me. That almost seemed funny. She added something like "you can decide what you want to know, or how much you want to know, or when you want to know it." That seemed almost funny too. There are holes in any landscape. Gaps where words should be. I learn something, forget it, then learn it again. Like Groundhog Day in Neuronville. Things happen and then are forgotten as if they hadn't happened. Or they are scribbled on scraps, then forgotten, as if they hadn't been scribbled on scraps.

One scrap said:

The right brain left

One scrap said:

I am under deconstruction

3

Reading is difficult. On my first try, I read "women on the Kansas frontier were subjected to plagues, thoughts and tropical ointments." Wow, women were subjected to plagues and "thoughts"? That didn't seem right, so I looked again and saw it said, "droughts." Next, I saw "commuter brain slides into creek," which really said, "commuter train slides into creek." I saw "thank you for your pitiful donation," which really said, "thank you for your pivotal donation."

I began working in media when I was in my twenties and magazine covers were painted on caves. Back then, we didn't have chatbots. We did the writing ourselves. This was before California exploded, followed by Oregon, Turkey, Europe, and Asia. On a good day, when winds were low, fires burned in place. Things burned every day. Countries, continents. We didn't chip, swipe, post, Insta, or battle identity theft. That was then. This is now.

The frontal lobes are among the most complex and recently evolved parts of the brain. They have vastly enlarged over the past two million years, which is like two seconds in evolution, about as long as it took to deconstruct mine. One moment and it was all gone. Being a mom, and a mom to my mom, and being me, and all the stories I would tell my grandchildren, if I have grandchildren — they atomized, terse and telegraphic, shot into space in a configuration that looked like *WTF*.

Words start coming back. Just not the right words at the right time. It's like I need nine ingredients for a recipe and I have three, or like I need twelve words for a thought, and I have five. I am missing the person who is my daughter or was my daughter, and maybe she is missing her mom.

Travel is challenging when you can't read instructions, decipher directions, or know if you've gone right or left. It's a huge deal for me when, a few years after the accident, I take Amtrak to Manhattan, then hail a speeding cab to meet my daughter for coffee. It takes everything I have. Or everything I have left.

4

She has chosen a cavernous coffee shop as loud and packed as a stadium. The line snakes in and out of velvet ropes, and everyone seems to be screaming. Before us, two girls prepare for an audition, while behind us, two guys do a postmortem on theirs. I am auditioning for the part of "normal mom," sort of like I was before. I want to walk like I did. I want to talk like I did. I want to think like I did. I am embarrassed by me.

Although supersonic jets are perfect for high-speed travel, you wouldn't want one to land in your head. But this is the impact most things make on my broken brain. During hours or minutes when I'm doing well, seeming "normal," it's like a door opens to let in some light, then slams me back to darkness again. My daughter has a brain-damaged mom who's shell-shocked by Manhattan and can't swipe a credit card.

I want to say this to my daughter:

I don't think you'll remember that day or a whole lot of other days we had. You sang "Part of Your World" from The Little Mermaid *— impromptu — in a packed school auditorium when you were three. A tiny body with a huge crystalline voice. Now I'm not part of your world. You won't remember how we were then, or the mom you had when you were one and two and three and four and five and six.*

You learned to talk.

You learned to walk.

We talked about birds and stars.

We were vibrant like peppermint ice cream.

Vibrant and alive.

Is there a certain number of memories my damaged brain can hold? Does making new memories push old memories out? If so, could we make a deal? I won't ask to make new memories, if you'll let me keep the old ones. Maybe ten or five or two?

Eighteen years post-truck, I ricochet between industrial-strength brain damage and the barely seeable kind, and still try to hide my mind, or at least the damaged parts. But I build homes for birds in which thousands of birds have been born. And I built a book with words.

My Take

I met Judith shortly after her accident, and even with her limited ability to communicate, what she wrote in that first workshop in Costa Rica blew me away! I understood not only that she had an important story to tell, but that she would be able to tell it in a fresh and powerful way. I could feel, because everything was a new beginning for her, that there would be an innocence about her voice. And I was right. When you reread it, I think you'll see what I mean.

To start with, you can't do better than that title: "Sorry Your Brain Broke. Here's a Casserole"!

Then "In my first life, I parked one word next to the other, and they stayed where I put them" is a great opening line. No one has ever written that sentence. I'll put money on it. And "parked" is the perfect word, considering what's coming next.

Judith sets up the situation right away by explaining she was a freelance writer and names some impressive credits.

Listen to the gorgeous rhythm of that next sentence: "I knew [1] where to start, [2] how to end, and [3] where to go in between." I'm in love with threes. I think there's an inherent power in the universe with threes: the father, the son, and the holy ghost; the three blind mice; three strikes, and you're out; three little words; pyramid power. And even jokes often feature threes — the punch line comes after the setup of three: "A priest, a rabbi, and an atheist walk into a bar. The bartender looks at them and says, 'What is this — a joke?'" Using groups of three things is not a writing rule. It's just what I love. And Judith has them everywhere. Watch.

The use of the past-tense "knew" makes us think, *Uh-oh! What happened?* We know something's up, but we need more. We want more.

The rest of the paragraph, with "the hits, the misses, the hissy fits, the highs, the lows, the pits. The hip little shake, the little hip shake..." — the whole thing is music. She plays with words, and you don't need to understand or question. You don't need any-thing but the play. But then she gives you real information about her former work when she says, "what raises hemlines, what raises heart rates." Wordplay is what advertising copy is all about, right?

Now here's a bit of brilliance: Look what she did with the "time," "life," and "people." You see how she didn't capitalize the names of the magazines? And then she corrected it, so she's subtly telling you she's still brain damaged.

Back to threes: staffer, freelancer, and "part-time ghost." Then "prevent," "protect," and "procure" — a three plus alliteration. Three *p*'s. Such lovely sound.

The next sentence, "all they wanted or needed to know, have, want, wear...," is an absolutely beautiful riff. Again she's playing. But every word is relevant. We get what she did for work. It's a great description in a few words of what you do when you are writing advertising copy.

Now comes the meat. What happened? More alliteration with "ten" and "Tuesday," then "truck." "Drunk," "stole," and "com-pressed" — all perfect word choices. When I read "compressed," I can't breathe.

The short sentence "I was in the car" all by itself! So powerful.

Now, when you read "My name is J. I used to have a name with more letters," you feel the loss. There it is right on the page.

The words "aphasia" and "amnesia" near each other are pow-erful. In explaining what they do, she uses the word "gouge," and you can actually feel the gouging. There are certain words that sing off the page. "Gouge" is one of them. There's not a writing-rule explanation for why one word is blah and another word vibrates.

Next, her list of everything she couldn't do and how she had to compensate by pointing is a perfect example of showing not telling.

What she did with "repurposed object" and "'repurposed' human" deepens the piece. We cannot do anything but feel for this narrator.

In "reconfigures any shards," do you hear what "shards" does? It's sharp. It cuts. It hurts. It's bits, not anything whole.

"Missed a step or a train or a decade" — another three. And going from things to "decades," as in time, tells you how long it's been.

"The phone weighs two hundred pounds. So does my right hand. My left hand weighs slightly less. My feet weigh slightly more." We can't even imagine what she's going through, so we need the exaggeration to feel how bad it must be.

"No one comes over to say, 'We're sorry your brain broke, so here's a casserole' " is so direct.

How about "I imagine my brain as a jigsaw puzzle of the United States"? A jigsaw puzzle would be brilliant enough, but do you see what adding "the United States" does? You need it for the rhythm. Then when she names what in the United States is gone, it's another showing not telling.

"They didn't come with a warranty. Neither did I." Wow!!!

With "What didn't blow up seems to break down," she incorporates opposites, which creates a nice balance. It's satisfying to the ear and the eye.

"Someone in scrubs puts more of something in the IV." Now we're in the hospital. This reminds us of how real this is. It's not conceptual. It's happening.

"Anti-aging, anti-wrinkle, anti-old. Perhaps it sucks out cellulite. Perhaps it just sucks." Playing with words. She's a pro.

"Some people are from another planet. Perhaps I am one of them." Another wow! And a possible insight.

She writes, "I imagined things," referring again to what she used to do as a professional writer. "Then something no one could imagine happened. Someone ran out of beer" — perfect way of conveying "drunk" — "and crushed a car that contained me." "Crushed" is a great visual that makes me think of the way people crush beer cans.

"Mighty chondria" instead of "mitochondria" is brilliant. It keeps us present in her confused brain.

Then she ends the paragraph with "Or not." No way can she make any definitive statements now that she's brain injured.

"Each step was a math problem." Has anyone ever anywhere put that combination of words together?

Equating "the odds of a sinkhole opening" with her finding the right word is powerful. In a sense, these are all reveals because she's letting you into her addled brain.

We wince once again with the play between "where language 'is held'" and "was held."

She repeats "jammed" to describe the different ways words got stuck inside her. I have said and will repeat a hundred times (more repetition, ha ha) that repetition when intentional works great. But repetition when you're being lazy weakens and dilutes the power of the term's original use.

Judith shows she's the queen of repetition with another one: "Not in alphabetical order, not in numerical order, not in chronological order, but out of order, like me."

"Like Groundhog Day in Neuronville" — a winner of a sentence! "I am under deconstruction" — another winner!

Her description of the difficulty of reading is another great "show, don't tell." We are in her shoes (broken brain) here.

"We didn't chip, swipe, post, Insta, or battle identity theft." She's showing how different things are now from when she was in the business.

"Two seconds in evolution, about as long as it took to deconstruct mine" reminds us how fast life can change, in case you, the reader, forgot and were thinking, *This stuff only happens to other people.*

"She has chosen a cavernous coffee shop as loud and packed as a stadium" gives us our first clue that the daughter is not sympathetic with the narrator's situation.

"I am auditioning for the part of 'normal mom'" is so painful. She's lost enough, and now this too?

"I want to walk like I did. I want to talk like I did. I want to think like I did" — "walk," "talk," and "think," all one-syllable words, have a nice sound, plus it's another great repetition and trio. And the saddest line of all: "I am embarrassed by me." Then the part where she describes her beautiful mothering job is heart-breaking too.

"I won't ask to make new memories, if you'll let me keep the old ones." How many of us have bargained with…who, God? The guys in charge of the brain?

Finally, she gives us a perfect ending, with "ricochet between industrial-strength brain damage and the barely seeable kind," followed by the redemption/triumph of the last two lines celebrating what she has built with birds and words.

 PROMPT: Take a memory and write a made-up version.

Dignity Cookies

Barbara Phillips

I'm a human rights advocate, having immersed myself a few years ago into the arena of the United Nations Universal Declaration of Human Rights and its opening words: "All human beings are born free and equal in dignity and rights. They…should act towards one another in a spirit of brotherhood." To deepen my understanding, I attended a small gathering organized by human rights activists from the Global South who explained that "rights" is the language of lawyers, while "dignity" is the language of the people. I embraced that distinction, wrote an essay advancing the importance of grounding our work in "dignity," and considered myself an adherent of that conceptualization. But, on a perfect October day in San Francisco, a bus ride that put me in proximity to homelessness shattered my understanding of myself.

Multitudes of people without homes survive on streets, parks, and vacant land in San Francisco, one of the most beautiful cities in the world. A recent count on a single night found seven thousand people surviving without homes. The condition of homelessness is an injustice violating every human right for which I am an advocate. All the conversations, conferences, and advocacy have failed to alleviate the suffering of unhoused people. I count myself among those struggling to understand why, so I turned to Bryan Stevenson, founder and executive director of the Equal Justice Initiative, for guidance.

I embraced his beautifully articulated insight and exhortation, "We cannot create justice without getting close to places where injustices prevail. We have to get proximate. There is power when we get proximate, and only then can we have mercy and compassion." His use of the word "proximate" in this way is unique and profound. "Proximate" is an adjective usually meaning closest in relationship, immediate, near, next, close. His use of the term grows out of his dignity-respecting relationships with his clients who suffer the worst of our criminal legal system, as he describes eloquently in his book *Just Mercy*. I applauded his insight and often repeated it during advocacy, along with the importance of "dignity."

On that perfect October San Francisco day, I boarded a bus in the financial district. What transpired stripped me of my delusion that I emulated Bryan Stevenson and those Global South advocates.

The first person I noticed was a weathered Black woman covered in layers of rags with a well-used backpack bulging at her feet as she sat in the first side-facing seat. It is not uncommon to find the homeless riding buses all day as simply a way to be. Given the opportunity to be proximate to her suffering from injustice, I sat at a distance. My thoughts were focused on sitting so that I could see what changes had happened to Market Street as we moved along. I took the space at the far end of the row of seats — as far away from her as possible while still being able to enjoy the streetscape. I stole glances at her as we moved along — the fragrance of a body only remotely acquainted with soap and water emanating from her. She looked so destroyed. I wondered what had brought her to this — being just a pathetic member of "the homeless."

As the bus moved along, two young white women boarded with a charming little boy. They took the first bench to my left facing forward. The pathetic woman couldn't take her eyes off the little boy. I became apprehensive. She began rummaging in her filthy backpack. *What in the world is she doing?* More apprehensive. Catching the little boy's attention, her face opened into a sweet smile and she, this woman who surely had nothing to spare, offered him a packet of store-bought cookies. I held my breath. Were those women going to let that little boy accept those cookies? Would I? The moment felt like eternity as I watched. The women looked at her, returned her smile, nodded to the little boy, and watched approvingly as he skipped over and thanked her as he accepted the treat. *Now, are they really going to let him eat that?* They opened the packet, and everyone ate cookies, smiling all the while at their generous benefactor.

I sat there masking my tears at being stripped of self-delusion. In that moment, I was forced to confront myself — that I believed in, advocated for, and wrote about human rights and dignity only in the abstract. No wonder there was no power to effect change in advocacy not grounded in mercy and compassion. Here on a bus in San Francisco were four people who lived the proclamation of the Universal Declaration. They understood inherent dignity and the part about "act[ing] towards one another in a spirit of brotherhood." They showed me what Bryan Stevenson is trying to get us all to understand. When I got on the bus, I had seen simply one of the thousands of "homeless" and distanced myself. But, in only a few minutes' time, I saw a kind, generous woman just beaming at all of us. And I joined in beaming right back and in the chatter till I got off at my stop with a gift far more valuable than those cookies.

 PROMPT: Write about a time you masked your tears.

Goodbye to All That

Nancy Slonim Aronie

My teacher, Ram Dass, used to tell a story about a guy who had a painting of a sunset: Most of the painting is blah, gray kind of nothing. But in the right-hand corner, there is a swath of magenta so electric, so brilliant, so breathtaking you don't even notice the blah. So the guy takes it to the framer, and two weeks later, he goes back and the framer says, "Gee, I didn't have a frame big enough, so I had to fold over…that pink thing."

I am listening for your audible gasp.

The reason I love this story is, over the years, I have realized that we're not in charge of much of what goes on in our lives. Husbands walk out, kids die, our best friends get cancer. But we are in charge of the size of the frame of our story. There is always tragedy, but there is *always* magenta.

So if you see only the gray, the depressing, the blah, you won't be able to get out of bed, and if you see only the magenta you're in la-la land. I know I've been writing a lot about balance and death lately. The middle way. Being able to feel broken and being able to celebrate with great joy, sometimes in the same minute.

I've been learning a bit about IFS, Internal Family Systems, a therapy that recognizes the many parts we have inside us.

And I have been accessing one of my scaredy-cat parts.

Two Sundays ago, I lost my brother-in-law. I loved the nineteen-year-old James Dean wannabe the minute I met him fifty-eight years ago. And this week I also lost a dear, dear friend.

I don't know about you, but when someone dies, aside from grieving, I'm always shocked. Part of me thinks, *How could this have happened?* But, of course, the logical part of me knows *Why* wouldn't *this have happened?* However, emotions are not logical, and emotionally I think when things are going along I expect them to continue going along. The scaredy-cat part of me doesn't want the change if things are great, and it's insisted that everyone will die except me and my close loved ones.

But because my close ones keep dying, either I have to amend my long-held fantasy or get real. That's where impermanence comes in.

Many years ago at Trinity College in Hartford, Connecticut, there were two Buddhist monks creating a mandala. It took three months for them to complete the piece of art. We were told the ancient ritual symbolizes the transitory nature of material life.

Crowds would come and watch in silence. Since I was working right there, I would go as often as I could.

I learned that one of the things the monks were doing was making the connection between their inner world and their outer reality.

And that the mandala is constructed to be dismantled immediately after it is finished.

I'll never forget when this absolutely exquisite mastery of color and texture was carried to the river and thrown in. Even though I knew that was supposed to happen, I was still shocked.

How could such perfection just be discarded like some piece of useless trash?

I remember standing on the banks of the Connecticut River and understanding that this was a brilliant illustration of the teaching that nothing is permanent. At the time, though, the teaching stayed in my outer reality. Intellectually I thought it was a great concept. But emotionally, I now know, I hadn't let it seep into my inner world.

It's so easy to forget about the swath of magenta when the blah is so *blah*.

Obviously it's time for my scaredy-cat part to find another mandala in the making.

"Our lives are written in disappearing ink."
— *Michelle Cliff*

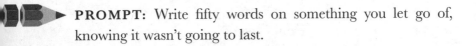

PROMPT: Write fifty words on something you let go of, knowing it wasn't going to last.

The Fawn

Justen Ahren

Two days into a cross-country trip with my estranged father, I woke with a fever and a sore throat. I stayed in bed watching the sunlight on the floor, listening to a tractor in the field. When it got close, I sat up and looked out the window. I saw my father on the John Deere. I hoped this man, whom I'd seen a few dozen times in my life, would stop and check on me. But he turned at the headland and went over the hill, mowing the June grass. My fever seemed to climb.

Four months before, on my twelfth birthday, my father called and asked if I wanted to drive to California with him that summer. This was the greatest gift I could've imagined. I'd always wanted to travel with him.

When I was six, my mother and I dropped him at the Pennsylvania Turnpike, and he hitchhiked to Oregon. I would not see him again for a long time. I went to my friend Mark's house afterward. He had a wall-sized map of the US in his bedroom. We took it down and I studied it. When Mark went downstairs to get us Tang, I lay on top of the map. My feet were in Pennsylvania. I stretched my body so my head touched Oregon.

We departed in June. I waited at the door for the Econoline van with a sunset painted on its sides to pull into the driveway.

My mother handed me spending money and a picture of her to keep in my wallet. "If you get homesick, kiss your pillow," she said. "I'll kiss mine." When we left, my father didn't look back, and neither did I.

We headed west, past Civil War battlefields. The first night, in sleeping bags on the roof of the van, eating graham crackers, and looking at the stars, my father said, "This is your journey into manhood."

I suddenly felt far away. Would this man, whom I barely knew, care for me? I think the tickle in my throat began then.

I must have fallen asleep listening for the tractor because I startled awake when the door slammed open and my father staggered into the room backward, holding something bundled in his shirt. His bare arms were sweaty. Bits of grass and daisy stuck to his shoulders and chest. He set the bundle on the bed next to me.

"I didn't see it!" He said, "It was hiding in the grass. Its mother must have been run off." He peeled the shirt back, and there was a fawn, frightened eyes, fur like sunlight on the forest floor, hooves the size of quarters, and then along its side, a red gash where the mower blade entered.

My father had stopped the bleeding, but the fawn needed a vet.

"I've got to finish mowing today if we are going to leave tomorrow." Then, noticing me, he placed his hand on my forehead. "You're burning up."

He got a white cooler from the van and unpacked its paper bags at the bedside. One by one he placed a bag on my chest and asked me to resist while he pressed down on my arm, which I held straight out. The first bag, my arm collapsed. The second bag was no better. But with the third bag, my arm remained strong against his pressure. "Echinacea," he said, and set it aside.

He tested a dozen bags on me — chamomile, cayenne, mullein, mint. He made a tea with the herbs that made me strongest. Then he returned to mowing, and I was alone with the fawn. I curled around it. I cried. We were in the same situation. "It's all right," I sang softly and repeatedly, and fell asleep.

The sun was across the room when my father returned. We drove to the vet. I wanted to go home, but I couldn't miss this opportunity to know him, for him to know me. I was afraid that whatever I decided, it would be wrong.

I drank another tea. And driving back to the cabin in the van with the painted sunset, my fever broke. The fawn slept on my lap. He was going to make it. He couldn't go back to his home. A friend of my father's would raise him. *I will cross the country with this man*, I thought. *I will make my journey into manhood. I will be afraid. But I can't go home.*

 PROMPT: Write about a time you couldn't go home.

This Is My Brain on Fire

Greg Anton

There was a sliver of a moon and a million stars when I went out to the backyard and made a small fire. Within an hour, when I looked up, it was as if the universe was folding in on itself.

I remember thinking, *How can the same person, with the same eyes, see things so differently after just eating a plant?* When I brought my gaze down from the black-and-white sky to the orange, red, and yellow fire, I'd never experienced the breathing, pulsating, perpetual motion of fire like that — Hieronymus Bosch faces appearing in a kaleidoscope of flames flicking in frenetic motion out of perfectly still logs. I visualized a hunter-gatherer woman carrying smoldering coals in a tree-bark burrito of moss, from cave to cave, keeping a traveling campfire going for weeks or months in her symbiotic relationship with nature. With that small bundle of coals and little else, she'd known that the more knowledge she carried in her mind, the less she had to carry in her arms. Of course that was before all the cerebral white men showed up lugging around oxcarts of lumber for square houses and propane tanks for patio barbecues.

Mushrooms have been growing on Earth for millions of years, I thought, *and eons before that, their spores floated around the universe looking for a warm, moist place to pollinate. Some societies made the mushrooms forbidden, but they don't care; they just keep growing. Tonight, on their forever journey to everywhere, carrying the DNA of the cosmos, they decided to plant their universal knowledge in the warm, moist place of my brain.* I looked back up at the sparkling sky. *This isn't something I just thought up; it's always been there waiting to be discovered.*

"I'm totally tripping out," I said aloud. My voice sounded like a stranger's.

I looked into the dark shadows. "Who's tripping out?" I said.

I jerked my head to the right. "Who said that?"

I jerked my head to the left. "Who's asking?"

I concentrated on the glowing coals. "I'm actually talking out loud, having a conversation with myself."

"It doesn't matter," I said to the fire.

"What doesn't matter?" I said.

"Exactly," I said and burst out laughing like it was the funniest thing I'd ever heard. Within a minute I knew I was laughing at himself laughing. My face flushed hot, tears ran down my cheeks, snot dripped out my nose. The laughing went on its own inertia for what seemed like a spooky amount of time until it finally quieted down to a sputtering chuckle.

I'd been bent over, head between my knees, and when I sat up, I thought, *Where am I?* Then I thought, *Who's asking all these questions?* The proverbial "I" had disintegrated along with my ego, and my usual patterns of cognition had dissolved into psychedelic mush. With nothing in my consciousness with enough footing to gain a purchase, not even sure I was conscious, I kicked off into an excavation of my subconscious that felt as risky as defusing a time bomb. I visualized shining a flashlight down dark basement stairs where a wild animal that feeds on fear crouched in the black crevice of my psyche and was so voraciously hungry that I conjured up an image of tossing down a two-inch-thick raw steak marbled with fat to pacify it. Then, without warning, my body of its own volition slowly started to stand up. It felt as if I could keep standing forever, an infinite, unfolding extendo-man, my head protruding above the wispy night clouds, up into the stars and beyond...bed, bath, and beyond. I picked up an infinitely long wooden pole, everything happening in super-slow motion enveloped in a warbly, low-end soundtrack like a slowed-down tape, sonorous bass notes physically pulsating in my ears. With the pole as tall as a tree, I proceeded to methodically spread out the coals. I slipped off my sandals and in super-slow motion, like everything, I walked with my hairy Sasquatch bare feet across the coals. Bright-orange neon light glowed between my toes, but my gaze stayed frozen into the middle distance.

I walked the length of the bed of glowing embers, turned around, stood motionless in the cool dirt, then walked back the way I'd come and sat down, my erector-set body folding in half and in half again. I sat in a lotus position and contemplated the blackened bottoms of my feet that were devoid of feeling, as if they were someone else's feet. I peered up into the hot night to the top of a giant redwood tree and realized we breathed in synchronicity — me breathing in oxygen, out CO_2; the tree, with its huge wooden lungs, doing the exact opposite. *What a setup*, I thought. *Who thought of that? But wait, how do mushrooms breathe without leaves? Wait? When? When do we wait? Do we wait while we're waiting? Does time only go forward?* I looked down, as if looking down a mile into the Grand Canyon, and when I reached into the depths to rub the bottoms of my feet, my hands felt more like puppets than hands.

Then I realized I was walking toward the coals again. I couldn't remember standing up. As I walked, I could feel the curvature of the earth. Now I was in a totally other dimension, hovering in a helicopter ten feet above my head, watching myself like I was watching someone else. With a white-knuckled grip on the joystick, I thought, *If that's me down there, who's flying this helicopter?* Then I heard a tiny inner voice: *Well, then, Mr. Fancy Pants, who's asking who's flying the helicopter?*

This was all happening in microseconds, and by some miracle of quantum physics, my brain connected linguistic protons to experiential electrons, and the noun *step* and the verb *step* melded into a single cell, as if colliding at the end of the two-mile-long Stanford particle accelerator. A red warning light went off in the cockpit with the word STEP! STEP! STEP! flashing on and off with buzzers and bells. The helicopter ran out of gas, the engine sputtered, the propellers locked up, the joystick went flaccid in my hand, and the helicopter crash-landed into the top of my head, breaking my concentration. I lost my balance with the sole of my right foot an inch from the fire, jerked back, steadied myself, put my foot down on the cool earth, and thought, *I could really burn my feet this time.*

 PROMPT: I could really burn my _____ this time.

A Day for Seeing Magic

Judith Hannan

It's 5:30 in the morning, and I'm trying to figure out if I want to kayak. The conditions are just the way I like them: calm and foggy. I just kayaked yesterday morning, like so many mornings and evenings, not just in summer, but in fall when the ducks return, in winter when I can break through the ice, in spring when the jellyfish bloom.

Today I am asking how motivated I am to paddle the same waters yet again. I get up to walk and feed the dogs, still not sure what my decision will be.

Each fall, after the holidays of Rosh Hashanah and Yom Kippur, a period of reflection and atonement, Jews reach the end of the Torah, the five books of Moses, only to start again from the beginning. The sages say that the reason we read the same words, year after year, is not that the text is different but that we come to it as different people, having grown and changed in some way during the past year.

I don't kayak for exercise. I do it for the sensation of the glide, of opening myself to an environment different from the one on land. So the questions I ask myself on this morning when I return with the dogs and prepare their breakfast are, *What about me is new? What might I see that either wasn't there the day before or that I hadn't noticed?* and *Who will I be upon my return?*

It is 6:15 by the time I pick up my paddle and walk down the path to Stonewall Pond, where I keep my kayak. The fog has thinned but still shrouds the view in a mist that, in a movie, would be accompanied by a tin whistle or bagpipe. Dew has settled on the meadow, turning the tall grasses into bejeweled fronds. Spiderwebs glisten as if painted with fairy dust. Today I am seeing magic.

The tide is on its way out, making for an easy coast under the bridge between Stonewall and Quitsa Pond. The green herons who were so still yesterday are feisty today, perhaps disturbed more by the great blue heron nearby than by me.

When I emerge from under the bridge, the moored boats are all facing me, as if waiting for my command to tell them their mission for the day or else in respectful greeting, bowing before me. I have become so used to seeing these boats as inanimate, separate entities that exist in relation to nothing else rather than as connected through the movement of the water and wind. I am surprised that I have imbued them with purpose, like the Disney cartoon characters in *Beauty and the Beast*. They might break into song at any moment.

The fog has thinned. It is getting hot. I used to wear a bathing suit when I kayaked and would stop and take a swim. When did I stop doing that and why? I ask the question but don't search for an answer. It's enough right now just to notice.

The fog is still settled in the area around Clam Cove. The boats have become ghost ships. They appear only as hints. Today is about enjoying blurred boundaries.

Out in Menemsha Pond I see a red boat, alone at its mooring, the line between sea and sky indistinguishable. It is clearly asking for its picture to be taken. I oblige and take some snaps.

It's a *Flying Dutchman* kind of day. My kayak and I could remain floating in and out of the mist all day and into the night, unseen by everyone except those looking for phantoms. This is a new image for me. The self I am right now is more inclined toward fantasy, a trait I rarely exhibit on land.

Yesterday morning was one filled with anticipation. I was awaiting the arrival of my younger daughter. My older daughter and son were already here, and this would be the first and last time all summer the three would be here on the island together. My strokes on the way back to shore were eager and made my arms sore.

This day, all three will be leaving, along with my grandson, my son-in-law, and his parents. Out on the water I am reclaiming my comfort with solitude. I cannot be reminded enough that I exist beyond motherhood while at the same time thrilling to the vision of my three beauties, marveling at the relationships they have with one another, which transcend my presence.

I rest often on the way back. There is no urgency, no reason to rush time. I drift, allowing myself to be pushed back by the tide. The water ahead of me glistens. A cormorant's head breaks the surface, and I realize I have seen very few of these birds this year. Where is yesterday's osprey, whose constant cry irritated my ears but today would offer a fitting soundtrack?

I haul my kayak up to its resting place, farther away from the water's edge than when I left. It is heavy, but I stay focused on one step at a time. I look down at my bare feet, see the nail scraped of its red polish from tripping yesterday on a rock. Today I am more mindful of where I put my feet.

I turn to face the pond as I always do before heading back to the house. I feel rooted, solid. My body is different, more accepting of the challenges I am presenting it with.

I am not a different person than I was yesterday. But by asking the question, I changed my intention, which altered my perspective. I am the same person thinking different thoughts. And, ultimately, having a flexible perspective is what keeps the world fresh for me each day.

 PROMPT: I am a different person than I was yesterday.

Keys to a Happily-Ever-After Divorce

Holly Nadler

The first reaction is when friends and acquaintances see us together — after long times apart — looking sprightly. And loving. And holding hands and greeting one and all as if we've just stepped away from our long-ago porch in East Chop, the steps facing nor'east over the Sound. They know we've been long divorced — was it really twenty years ago? — so they're shocked to see us looking like we've just returned from our honeymoon. Was that really forty-three years ago?

They ask if we're back together again. My ex, whose name is Marty, says, "We were never apart!" Close friends know he's joking. They've heard him answer the same question with "Are you outta yer f**king mind?!" But, digging deeper, most of the familiar faces we encounter comment on their own experiences with divorce, and they share info such as this: "My ex hates me. Absolutely hates my guts."

Have Marty and I ever hated each other, much less each other's guts? No. We made the decision to give up bicoastal living, which was here on the Vineyard and way out west in Hollywood, as it had grown too costly. We decided to plump for the island, where our son, Charlie, about to enter second grade, could receive a traditional childhood, we felt, with seasons and safe streets and family friends who stood outside on those same porch steps to sing Christmas carols. But we bumped up against...guess what? Real life and real jobs. Marty helped his friend Peter White at his Old Stone Bakery — "Time to make the doughnuts," my husband would drone when he left the house at five in the morning — and I received a real estate license and motored into Edgartown every day, noon and night, to pull in some big-girl bucks. Well, I hope I can explain this properly, but we two neurotic creatives, set free from the West Coast, felt suddenly overwhelmed by anxiety caused by weird stuff like mortgage payments and a mounting tax bill, and what happened to us was entirely human: We grew morose. And aloof. That's the worst you could say about us.

We know now, looking back, that the marriage could have been saved had we made a concerted effort to plow through these challenging times together. But we weren't up to the task. We were too immature. Marty's success in show biz had come early, interfering with a clear understanding of life — still in his twenties, he went from stand-up comedy to working on hit shows such as *Happy Days* and *Laverne & Shirley* — and I was a spoiled Valley girl. Yeah, *that*

Valley. The San Fernando Valley just over the mountains from Los Angeles. The one that gave the original rep to lazy sluts like me.

After a number of heart-to-heart talks when we pledged to keep trying, we finally lost our nerve and sought to try no longer. We appeared with our lawyers before a judge at the Edgartown courthouse. My lawyer, who'd looked back over Marty's earnings from studio jobs, wanted to go for alimony. At the time I was making a fairly good living from real estate and some writing breaks, such as an article in *Lear's* magazine touching on my experience with popping testosterone to keep me from weeping after big meetings. This article turned into an option from Touchstone Studios to make a movie out of the story. So I said "No! No! No!" to the alimony demand, thinking of poor Marts heading out at first light to make the doughnuts.

I'm still proud of my choice.

As we descended the wide white cement stairs of the courthouse, we linked arms and decided to go out for dinner that night. Not exactly to celebrate but to mark the occasion. We headed later on for that darling restaurant in Edgartown, Atria. Marty told the elegant lady behind the counter, "Don't bother with a romantic table. This morning we got divorced."

We stayed close insofar as we bought a brand-new family house just outside Oak Bluffs, where we resided as congenial roommates until our son shoved off for college, nearby at Boston University. Even though both of us were ostensibly dating, we also found time to rub each other's backs as we watched *The Sopranos* together in Marty's den. I wrote books about island ghosts and hosted haunted-house walking tours in the summer. I also published books of ghost stories and other subjects of local interest, while Marty got hired on big movies such as *Pretty Woman* and *Runaway Bride* in a capacity called "on-set writer," as in, the director would hand over the script and say, "Nadler, can you take this scene to your hotel room and punch it up?" (In other words, make it funnier.)

We sold the house, and I turned over my share to start a bookstore in Oak Bluffs, which rode the tides for six years all the way up to the recession of 2008. Meanwhile, Marty and I still ran into each other in town, both of us with big grins on our faces and eager to catch up. Then one day Marty sat me down on a bench outside the Cousen Rose Gallery and told me he was forfeiting his year-round rental nearby and settling into the Florida condo inherited from his mother. I cried the whole time, proud of my actress-y ability to keep from grimacing as tears coursed down my cheeks. Meryl Streep would have been jealous. After twenty minutes, I asked if my mascara was still in place. It was. Thank the lord for waterproof! We both confessed we were done with this sad talk.

There were no more sad talks. And finally we made plans to meet now and then as if we were still stably married oldsters. I'd fly down to Florida over New Year's and spend a couple of fun weeks. In the last ghastly period of time we met during the pandemic, we touched base with friends in Asheville, North Carolina, sometimes watching the news, trying to make sense of it all, and taking heart and gaining strength from being together. Out of this came people asking, "Are you back together?" We'd shrug and chuckle.

The best part is when we're in company and able to share funny stories from — yowzers! — like forty years ago. For instance, the other night over dinner at my senior-housing apartment — I call it my "hermitage" — we reminisced about long-ago days at the Improvisation Comedy Club in Los Angeles. We lived out at the beach and faced a long drive home, which led me to say to Marty, "Can we leave? People are talking too loudly and smoking, and I can't take it any longer." At the end of the bar, Marty said in his Bronx comic's strident voice, "Attention, everybody! Can you please stop talking and stop smoking? My wife has had it with the noise and the smoke and wants to go home!"

To which another comic at the other end of the bar said in an equally grating voice, "Tell the [expletive describing a part of the female anatomy] to WAIT OUTSIDE!!"

How many couples who've been dating in the past few years or weeks can dredge up tales from back in the days when we didn't even have cellphones?

So at this very moment as I write about our weird little divorce, Marty's visiting me at the hermitage. We sleep together in my brand-new queen bed with my sweet rescue doggy who loves to nestle between us and burrow into Marty's neck and then his butt. TMI? All I can say is that for dating couples, the capacity to get intimate with one another's pets is a sign of, if not lasting happiness, then happiness for now.

Here's the key: If you loved each other in the first place, you can glom onto those things that first grabbed you, particularly if they're good things, such as a bang-up sense of humor, kindness, and a shared aspiration to change the world. For the better. That's gotta be done right now, as we're all aware. My beloved exhusband and I have this natural urge to evolve and to goad each other on in this endeavor. Therefore, should we never have parted ways? Naw. We both appreciate our time alone. In our dotage, alone time is easier to negotiate from divorce than a long-term marriage. At this advanced age, alone time allows us to take the necessary steps on our spiritual journeys that lead to whatever liberation we can muster. And then, whenever we spend precious time together, we encourage the other to reach for the sky. With joined hands. Amen.

Can I get an amen from my ex? Keep listening. His hearing has faltered, along with, well, everything else.

 PROMPT: Write a happy divorce piece. Make it up if you must.

Be Vulnerable

*I*n my classes, I say right at the beginning that vulnerability is the element I value most in the personal narrative. It will invite me into the story. I need to know you feel, you hurt, you are insecure just like me. If you are the expert and you don't show me your broken heart — that you have been mortified at a dinner party when your breast milk leaked all over your silk blouse, that you gossiped about someone who was standing within earshot, that you congratulated someone on being pregnant and realized too late she had just gained some weight — I can't find myself in your story. Tell me we are sisters in shame. Tell me you are my perfectly imperfect brother from another mother. Our details may be totally different, but you can lead me to share your feelings about what happened. Then I'm with you every step of the way. You don't have to be a victim for me to relate to you. You can come out shining, successful, victorious, but somewhere in the piece let me know you are human. You failed. You screwed up. You were lost. I find it very sad when people say about someone grieving, "She's so strong, she hasn't shed a tear." That's not strong to me. Vulnerability is strength. Show me your heart, and I'll follow you anywhere.

Dinner at Our House Was...

Susan Joyner

Dinner at our house was on green Naugahyde chairs, an easy wipe for piss and smashed peas.

We sat around a frail cherry dining table that now sits in the garage of my childhood home, covered in stacks of unused Depends, left behind when my mother finally left with what remained of her mind.

She was a bitter housewife of the Southern '60s. Mama loved her *Ms.* and *Mother Jones* magazines but was a reluctant mother who let me know that she had wanted to be a motorcycle-riding editor in New York City.

Instead, she made pot roasts and mashed potatoes, and we sat quietly awaiting our father's verdict that the food needed more salt.

My mother was full of salt, shaking it into my wounds of inadequacy. "You must really like the school cafeteria food. Those pants are not becoming on you."

She was the unofficial editor of my life.

An A paper from school met her red pen, and I went from writer to failure. Same for a letter sent home from my freshman year in college — she returned it covered in red, changing my desperate attempt to sound smart with my description of doing "various assundry" things to the correct "various *and* sundry." Who knew? Not me. My English-major plans seemed a sham, so I switched to psychology and chemistry, where I felt safer from the pen.

Later, I was a third-year medical student doing a pediatric rotation at a nearby hospital. But something in me was changing. I was slipping from my ways of effortful well-being into a state of numbness. One of my patients was a critically ill two-year-old, and the child and her family broke my heart. When the attending asked me for lab results on rounds, I stared blankly. At a radiology conference, I was called on to interpret the results of a barium enema. The presenter handed me a laser pointer. I glanced at the film, handed back the laser pointer, and walked out of the room and to my car. Back at my apartment, I sat on the floor, drinking cheap red wine and watching squirrels eat birdseed on the rotting deck.

After a stay in a psychiatric hospital, where I was further numbed by a bevy of antidepressants, my mother sent me a package. My heart leaped. Perhaps she loved me after all. In it was M. Scott Peck's book *The Road Less Traveled*. I opened it to find that Dr. Peck's work had been heavily edited. There were marked-out words, corrected punctuation, and long columns of editorial disagreement in the margins. All done by my mother. At least Dr. Peck got the red pen treatment too.

I had also done my own editing, trying to remove all my many unacceptable parts — my anguish, my rage, my deep sense of worthlessness — by becoming a doctor, an identity that I thought would make me impervious to red marks. Yet I was just a crusty carapace, moving through the world with a forced smile, my inner pool of blood the red ink of my mother's pens; hers the red ink of her father's harsh words. And now it's time to bleed.

My Take

From the first paragraph in Susan Joyner's piece, I feel the tenderness and sensitivity of the writer. And I am worried for her.

She wrote the piece in response to my very first prompt at a workshop at Kripalu in Stockbridge, Massachusetts.

She writes "green Naugahyde" in the first line. It conveys texture and color, and I love colors. This specific detail gives me a visual right off the bat.

"Frail" is a great word to describe the cherry table. I know it's not solid, and it might even be a metaphor; we shall see. Another vivid detail.

I think good writing is so much about how the words sound. Yes, word choices. Yes, rhythm. Yes, story. But listen to the sound. The alliteration of "piss" and "peas" is music.

"Unused Depends!" OMG. It reminds me of that six-word

flash-fiction story often attributed to Hemingway: "For sale: baby shoes, never worn."

Then the word "finally" in "my mother finally left with what remained of her mind." Look at the implication. In one word, we get that this woman did not go gently into that good night.

"Bitter" and "housewife" are perfect word choices.

More alliteration: "Southern '60s."

By using the word "Mama," the author reinforces the Southern thing, but more importantly she doesn't have to say the word "mother" twice. I'm big on trying to not repeat words near each other unless you are doing it for emphasis. Unintentional repetition weakens the initial use. So if she had written "mother" instead of "mama" and then "mother" again, it would have diluted the power of its first use.

Ms. and *Mother Jones* not only give us a time frame but let us know the woman is a feminist or was trying to be one. She didn't hide her lost dreams. She made her daughter know she wanted to be a "motorcycle-riding editor" and how much she had sacrificed for this shitty job she finds herself in now. So instead of relishing being a mom, she lets the kid know she's made a compromise and isn't living her dream.

And don'tcha want to read on? I did!

Instead of just saying "dinner" she names the dinner: pot roast and mashed potatoes. We need specific details like this. If you can't remember the exact food, make it up. But be sure not to name a food that became popular twenty years after your story takes place. Like avocado toast. Or chicken tagine.

"We sat quietly awaiting our father's verdict that the food needed more salt" — what's that about? Look how much we learn in one sentence about the relationship between the husband and wife. He's a harsh critic. Are we afraid at this table? Yes, we are afraid. Here's a piece of the vulnerability. Here the reader feels for the narrator.

And this is interesting: Up till now, I hate this mother. But suddenly here I feel a bit for her. More vulnerability. Because I relate to not wanting to be cooking pot roast and mashed potatoes for... *Who are these people in my house anyway?* I want to be riding on the back of James Dean's motorcycle with my long auburn tresses blowing in the wind and accepting my Academy Award wearing my Oleg Cassini full-length organdy gown. *I just want to thank my mom...*

"My mother was full of salt, shaking it into my wounds of inadequacy." This is a gorgeous line, powerful. Do you feel the willingness of the writer to share her hurt?

Then the quote: "You must really like the school cafeteria food. Those pants are not becoming on you." Now I hear her mother, not through interpretation but directly. Let me hear people speak (see Secret 5, "Use Direct Quotes"). I will know them better if I hear their words. I will hate them or love them better if I hear their words. And I've lost my empathy for her mother here. How can you do that to your child?

"She was the unofficial editor of my life." A great metaphor, plus it's literal.

"An A paper from school met her red pen." "Met" is the right word here. "I went from writer to failure." This amplifies the vulnerability in the piece. To me, *vulnerability is the most important element in a personal essay*. I'm sorry if I repeat myself. But this is a big one for me.

Her vulnerability makes us pissed at this broken mother, furious that she has shamed her daughter, and our hearts are filled with support and unconditional love and caring for the girl who didn't get what she was supposed to get: a cheerleader.

"Same for a letter sent home from my freshman year in college — she returned it..." Returned??? OMG! No, please no! "Covered in red" — ahh, there it is. That could be the title of the piece.

She continues: "changing my desperate attempt to sound smart with my description of doing 'various assundry' things to the correct 'various *and* sundry.' Who knew? Not me. My English-major plans seemed a sham, so I switched to psychology and chemistry, where I felt safer from the pen."

Lots of gems here. First, the word "desperate" is perfect. It's visceral. Imagine feeling desperate to sound smart to impress your own mother. My heart hurts here.

"Assundry" is absolutely killer! How many of us wrote what we thought we heard? In the Christmas carols, the famous "Round young version" and "O come, lettuce, adore him" — same thing. Once again we can relate. And we must relate to this author.

"I felt safer from the pen." This reminds me of a quote by the writer Isaac Babel: "No iron can pierce the heart with such force as a period put in just the right place."

And then we have "sham," "switched," "psychology," and "safer." Do you hear all those *s* sounds?

Next, we fast-forward: "Later, I was a third-year medical student." Whoa, what happened? Total switcheroo. Survival. *Maybe she'll love me if I'm a doctor.*

"But something in me was changing. I was slipping from my ways of effortful well-being into a state of numbness." Numbness. Uh-oh. Look what abuse does. Plus, we have "changing," "slipping," and "being." I love when there are a bunch of *-ing*s together. They sing off the page. And the rest of the paragraph shows, not tells, about what the numbness did.

"After a stay in a psychiatric hospital" — yikes! The story deepens, drops into the underbelly of what happens when a broken person breaks another one. We are surprised, and we are also not surprised. But we are suffering. Because we already care so much about this narrator. More vulnerability.

Her mother sends the M. Scott Peck book *The Road Less Traveled*, also with a multitude of her corrections. And the narrator injects dark humor and sarcasm with the line: "At least Dr. Peck got the red pen treatment too."

The whole last paragraph is gorgeously vulnerable. "I had also done my own editing, trying to remove all my many unacceptable parts — my anguish, my rage, my deep sense of worthlessness — by becoming a doctor, an identity that I thought would make me impervious to red marks." Here, she brings us back to the red marks — just perfect!

"Yet I was just a crusty carapace," she writes. "Crusty" is a great descriptive word — hard and brittle. And "carapace"! Now our writer is just a hard outer shell of a person. Hollowed out. With a defensive covering. Which is what happens to us when we are hurt over and over again. This is universal. Universal is important (see Secret 7). Our details may be different, but the shame, the rejection, the results of being abused are the same.

She's "moving through the world with a forced smile." How many people do we all know who have a phony smile covering the pain and the fear inside? And did you ever have one of those?

With "my inner pool of blood the red ink of my mother's pens; hers the red ink of her father's harsh words," the writer tells us what made her mother so brutal — surprise, surprise. So even though we are still on the side of the writer, we go back to a tiny bit of empathy, knowing the mother got shafted too.

The last line, "And now it's time to bleed," could mean it's time for the writer to feel again. To let go of the numbness and take the chance (because she got this story out of her body and onto the page) of feeling her long-held sorrow, of releasing all the blood that had hardened inside her.

 ► **PROMPT:** The buck stops here.

Lost and Bedazzled

Mirabai Starr

As you allow the grandeur of the world to break through your habitual perceptions, your appreciation for the rest of creation grows more personal. You begin to envision the earth as a beloved relative and nurture an intimate relationship with her. You worship the body of the world. You'll do anything to make her feel safe and happy. Your holy wonder gives rise to a fierce protectiveness and a bold desire to act on her behalf. This care comes with pain. You cannot bear to see animals suffer, gas pipelines ravaging the wilderness, aquifers drying up. Your pain is in proportion to your love.

Like a sabbath practice, connecting with the earth takes effort. Ever since I was a child, I have had an irresistible urge to wander alone by streams, in deserts and snowfields, beaches and orchards. I scramble up boulders and slide down arroyos. I hike up ridges and sit beneath ponderosas. I rub sagebrush between my fingers and inhale every single time I take my daily walk through the high desert where I live. Time in nature is as essential to my well-being as sleep. Which is ironic because I have the worst sense of direction on the planet. How could someone so bedazzled by the world be so helplessly lost in it? I climb a mountain one way, and it looks completely different on the way back down. I have led friends and relatives the wrong way on paths I have taken a hundred times. Or stopped in the midst of guiding someone back from a long hike to a favorite overlook, convinced that we were on the wrong trail, when in fact that was the only path back out; it just felt wrong.

I do not trust my instincts. (You shouldn't trust my instincts either.) The world enchants me, the earth captivates me, and I consistently turn left when I should have turned right.

It all feels so fluid to me. Like a river that meanders and never stays the same. I wish I could say this is OK with me, but it still causes me great angst when I try to drive out the parking lot of a shopping center and have no idea which way to point my car. I have burst into tears more than once finding myself hopelessly turned around on city streets, on mountain trails, and in museums. Like something fundamental is broken in me, something regular people take for granted. Of course, there is no such thing as an unbroken person. We all have secret places where some faculty we are certain was properly installed in everyone else just doesn't seem to work in us. The invitation is to connect with the beauty at the heart of the wound, the gift inside the deficit, the holiness available in the hole.

I suppose I have other senses that compensate for my lack of a sense of direction. A capacity for my heart to be broken open by a coyote crossing the highway at sunset. A tendency to be silenced by the silence of falling snow. The way I feel music in the cells of my belly. A certain fearlessness in the presence of dying people and grieving people. An impulse to bear witness to suffering. To see pain as art.

 PROMPT: Write about your sense of direction.

Dinner at Our House Was...

Suzy Trotta

Dinner at our house was a crapshoot. It depended a lot on whether my dad was sober or my mom thought she was dying again or not.

If everyone was alcohol- and imaginary disease–free, we had wonderful Southern dinners at the kitchen table in our eighty-year-old house in the country. Think skillet-fried chicken and skillet corn, chicken-fried steak and mashed potatoes from scratch, and a lot of homemade biscuits and corn bread.

The food was delicious, but my parents both chain-smoked, and my father would often smoke while he ate, using his plate as an ashtray. As a tightly wound child, I did not like that, but my attempts at asking him to stop went unheeded. He also made hungry bear noises that both scared and appalled me.

If my dad wasn't sober, it meant that he wasn't home and also that my mother was either suffering from a new ailment — telling me how we had to leave the house and finally be free of Dad (even though she would be wildly in love with him again three days later when he got home) — or not talking to me due to something I had done, though I could never quite figure out what.

On these nights, I was on my own. I became quite a good little chef. My two favorite things to cook were Hamburger Helper — Cheeseburger Helper if I was feeling fancy — and deep-fried anything. We had a FryDaddy, which was a large deep fryer that we kept in the fridge. My mother reused the oil over and over again, so it was heavy when I hauled it out onto the counter. The big white block of fat inside would take over an hour to heat up, but I would watch one of our three channels on our tiny black-and-white TV with the rabbit ears, salivating at the thought of the French fries or redneck donuts — fried canned biscuits with powdered sugar on top — that I would soon enjoy.

In retrospect, I'm sure it's fine to let an eight-year-old run a deep fryer. I was certainly tall enough to reach the counter without a stool, and I took proper precautionary measures, like making sure the oil was bubbling and spitting up out of the fryer before dumping in the food.

I honestly think I enjoyed my dinners alone more than the ones with my parents. Even though I didn't know the specifics of their dynamics at the time — that my father was an alcoholic and my mother was a crazy-ass hypochondriac — I still felt the tension, and I could never relax and really enjoy those biscuits. But if I made Cheeseburger Helper, I enjoyed the whole skillet all by myself, often in the company of Barney Miller or Hawkeye Pierce. It makes me hungry and a little homesick just thinking about it.

 PROMPT: Dinners alone

Here's Why You Have to Make Up with Your Siblings

Nancy Slonim Aronie

Right before my sister died, we had the biggest fight we had ever had. I thought, *She's gonna die and we're gonna not be speaking.*

Here it is two years later, and even though I can't remember what the fight was about, I know it was huge and that she took her time accepting my apology. But thank God she finally melted and we fell into each other's arms and cried.

Anyway, today while walking in the woods, I smelled that mixture of dead leaves decomposing and new life buds on the trees. The daffodils alrcady gone. Just the beginning of spring where March wouldn't let go and pass the torch and April didn't want to play ball.

All of a sudden, I saw a crinkled-up piece of cellophane, and it looked just like the wrapping of the shortbread cookies of my youth, Lorna Doones. My husband would have picked up the piece of trash. All I did was take a deep dive into a memory of my father flipping out over the fact that the whole bag of cookies was gone. "Who ate the last one?" I could hear him yelling. I remember I lied and said, "*I* did, Daddy." I always tried to protect my sister, whose weight had become a thing the two of them argued over.

The more I thought about it, the more I wasn't sure if I actually had confessed to eating the last cookie or if I was glad she was getting yelled at and not me. Now I was wondering if he was upset because of the calories or the money or that we would spoil our dinner.

That was always our mother's big line. "Don't eat before dinner. You'll spoil your appetite." That memory is the kind of thing my sister and I would be cracking up over now.

I thought, *I will call her and ask, (1) "Did Daddy really flip out over the Lorna Doones?" And (2) "Did I step up for you?" And (3) "Do you remember how they always said, 'Don't eat. It will spoil your appetite'?"*

There I was in the woods with an entire theater piece going on in my head, and then the shard ripped across my heart. *I can't call her. She's dead.*

So, not only are we not going to have any more of the laughs we had as adults, over our parents and all our stupid early-childhood stuff, but I also am not going to get answers. Because no one else can corroborate. No one has the shared memories we have. Who will remind me of who I used to be? Who will finish my sentences with the exact right words? There are so many things that still sting…

Like a few weeks ago when I was making Indian pudding. The first time I ever tasted that delight, it was 1963 in Maine. I was visiting my newly married sister, and she was cooking the pudding on a wood stove. A wood stove!! Whoever heard of such a thing? We grew up in suburbia with wall-to-wall carpeting. Now she was living in a funky farmhouse with the intoxicating smell of burning wood. Did she add vanilla or almond extract? I want to call her. But I…

Like how our parents made us wait an hour after eating before they'd let us so much as dip a toe into the water's edge, let alone swim. Everyone in the world was splashing, jumping, screaming for joy while we sat on our stupid towels waiting, waiting, waiting. An hour to a nine-year-old is a lifetime.

You know how badly I want to call you-know-who and bitch and moan together and talk about how differently we raised our kids? We would say almost in unison about our own parents, "They did the best they could." And then admit there were some "bests," like when our father would come home from work and say, "How was school? Did you walk or take your lunch?" And we would all crack up.

Yes, I want to talk to my sis. But dammit…

This morning my friend Ray called and was complaining about his sister who he hasn't spoken to in three years.

I get it. She was awful to him. But I know if my sister and I hadn't resolved our thing, my heart would have two gashes instead of just the one.

I'm not saying it's easy. But I know people who have done it. And they will tell you it takes work. So if you are in a similar situation with a sibling, Dr. Aronie says, *do the work*.

My sister would say, "If you don't get it done this lifetime, you'll be back."

I say, don't count on it.

Do it now.

 PROMPT: Write a letter to a sibling or someone you should really reconcile with.

Tell Me about What Is Broken

Beverly Pincus

Things break:

When I was seven, my very beloved piggy bank, which wasn't a pig, but a dog, named Brownie. My father got him for me, just because. I loved that he did that. My brother got mad at me. I don't remember for what — I often don't remember the cause, just his rage, which intensified as we got older until it spilled onto me in violent slaps and punches. He shattered Brownie — just like our filial bond got shattered — and it was hard to reconcile the sweet boy of our childhood with the lost, angry, brooding young man he became, and still is.

My glass unicorn on its real sterling-silver chain. My father got this for me too, when I was eight, at a souvenir stand at Rye Playland. The best kind of day, sunny with a light breeze and rides and cotton candy and time alone with my dad. We had an inside joke about unicorns after he'd stood up to my first-grade teacher who modified a poem I wrote about one, adulting my writing by changing the critical last line from stating definitively that I saw a unicorn to saying there is no such thing. I was crushed and crying, and my father spoke to her in a no-nonsense way, admonishing her that she was never to squelch my creativity again. He was my hero and my first love, and when I was ten, he threw himself off the roof of a building, and that was that. His body broken and my happiness with it. I wore the unicorn as a reminder of him until the day two years later when the clasp gave out and it slipped from my neck and shattered on the floor, and I felt I had lost my father all over again.

The chair in the living room when I was five and was playing on it the way I wasn't supposed to, holding the arms tightly for support and doing a backflip. I heard the wood crack and suddenly was on the floor, and I was so scared I would be spanked for my naughtiness. I went to my mother tearfully and confessed, and surprisingly she did not punish me, saying she saw how bad I felt and that was punishment enough. I still remember that, how I was redeemed.

When I was nineteen my heart broke, and forty years later it still feels that way when I think of Yuval, my Israeli beloved with the huge brown eyes dark as Turkish coffee, who smelled of grapefruit citrus from the orchards, and mud and sweat and apple soap. I picked grapefruit in the orchards too, and he would playfully shake my ladder and call up that he would catch me if I fell. We ate avocado spread on toast for breakfast, conjugated verbs in Hebrew in the afternoons, and made sweet love at night. Then one day he fell asleep at the wheel of his tractor and crashed it into a ditch, and all that ended when he was lowered into the ground. I held a rose in my hand and twisted its thorns into my palm until it bled as the rabbi recited Kaddish, the Jewish prayer for the dead. Hearts do break; it's not just a myth.

My wrist when I was twelve and was visiting my friend Natalie for the weekend and we were riding bikes and I fell off mine. I thought I even heard the bone crack. Three boroughs away my mother, stirring the soup, stopped cooking when she had the vision of me falling and rushed to the phone to call Natalie's mother to see if I was all right, even before they had a chance to call her from the hospital. I often think of that, how she knew, and the inextricable bond that is between mother and child, that comes from growing in another's body. My mother now is ninety and elegant and aged, and as I watch her sleep at night and match my breath to hers, I wonder how much longer I will have her — weeks, months, years? — and how when she is gone I will be an orphan and yearn for her soft voice and sound advice and delicate laughs, and how the emptiness without her will be a brokenness too.

 PROMPT: Write about something broken.

What I Didn't Tell You

Jim Murrin

I didn't tell you that I was entirely spent before you departed.

That I missed your touch, that I had forgotten your laughter, even your smile — any positive gesture, any conversation — that life as I knew it had ended.

I didn't tell you that your darkness swallowed me whole.

That I was smothering and haunted.

That I hated your self-medication and your deceit.

That I was horrified by your threats to end your life — but never thought you would.

You said, "I would kill myself if I knew I wouldn't fail" — it seemed abstract until you did.

I didn't tell you — when the coroner was finished, Alex and I went together to view your frozen body. I was overwhelmed and had to leave the room. Alex spoke to you alone. I returned and kissed your forehead and opened your eyelid and gazed into your eye.

I didn't tell you
...that I read the autopsy report. That they dissected you and photographed you.
...that they weighed your heart (245 grams) and your brain (1,265 grams).
...that they recorded your eyes as hazel — but I knew they were blue.
...that they even measured the furrow in your neck (a quarter-inch deep, two inches from the base of each ear).

I couldn't tell you — they said your heart and brain were normal.

 PROMPT: What I didn't tell you then...

The Hardest Thing

Nicole Galland

The hardest thing is other people's kitchens. And also their bathrooms and hallways and light switches and guest beds and guest-bed pillows, and coatracks and mudrooms and parking and thermostats and TV habits and whatever shelf or cupboard or table is closest to the door. And laundry. And pets. And rules about pets. And wifi passwords. And what lights stay on and off when. And rules about locking the house. And in the bigger picture, the nearest drugstore, supermarket, vet, ATM, post office. One-way streets and parking regulations. And how long does it take to get from this specific place where I am staying today, to my rehearsal, to the ferry, to my lunch meeting, to the doctor's, to the dentist's?

But most of all, the hardest thing is other people's kitchens. How do they stack their dishes in the dishwasher, and how well should I rinse off the crumbs first? It's different in each household. Do they compost? How do they sort their recycling? Which is the silverware drawer? Where might I find a colander? What do I do if their knives are dull? Do they have paper towels, and what do they get used for in this household? Can I help myself to cooking oil? To breakfast? To milk for my tea? Should I be buying vegetables only for myself or for the household? When they ask if I'd like an omelet or a salad or a cup of soup, are they just being hospitable or do they mean it? It's different in each household. Where can I plug in my yogurt maker so it won't be in the way or get accidentally unplugged when they make their morning smoothie or evening popcorn or charge their phone? Do they reuse Ziploc bags? Where are their spices? Do they have turmeric? Do they mind the smell of cumin? Of kimchi? Of tuna fish? Where should I put the dog's water bowl and food? Can I invite friends over for a cup of tea? A meal? If I cannot abide the state of the countertop, will they feel judged if I scrub it right in front of them? Or is it more insulting if I do it furtively when they're not looking? When I empty the dishwasher, where do I put the things I can't find homes for? Which spatula is safe to use on their expensive-looking high-tech pan? Where should I store my almond butter? Do they refrigerate their soy sauce? It's different in each household. The brain that desperately needs to be writing a five-hundred-page novel is overwhelmed by the exhaustion of having to learn, and then re-learn, all these other people's kitchens.

 ► **PROMPT:** Write a piece about what you have experienced as a long-term or just an overnight guest.

College Essay

Brad Hamermesh

Thanks to post-traumatic amnesia, there is a five-week period of my life that I don't remember.

I'm happy I don't remember hitting the tree. I'm glad I have no memory of lying alone in the ER. I'm relieved I don't remember the chest tube. I'm grateful I don't remember the pain of eight freshly fractured bones. I'm most thankful that I can't recall my family sobbing at the sight of my broken body.

On February 20, 2020, a skier saw me lying by the side of a trail, called ski patrol, and a team of first responders rushed me into a helicopter that transported me to Children's Hospital Colorado.

I was nonresponsive and relying on a ventilator to breathe. I suffered a traumatic brain injury, broken bones, and a lacerated lung. When I woke up two days later, the left side of my body was paralyzed. My future was uncertain.

I have no recollection of my time at Children's. I don't remember sitting up, standing for the first time, or relearning to walk. Nor do I remember having surgery to repair my lung or being in the "flight stage" and constantly wanting to escape.

I've seen pictures of myself on a hospital bed with tubes coming out of every part of my body and videos of therapists walking my legs for me. I've watched the first video that I took telling my mom I love her. I have no memory of any of it, yet I know it happened, and I know that my response was to persevere. To this day, I always keep my head up because I know that I can. Because I did.

The memories that I do have stick with me.

I remember my first occupational therapy session at Spaulding Rehabilitation Hospital in Boston. The therapist told me simply to move my left arm. Looking at the limb, feeling like I was trying to lift a car with one hand, I couldn't even budge it.

I realize that nothing should be taken for granted.

I remember looking up at the ceiling in my net-protected bed, unable to picture my future. I couldn't have guessed I would run a 10k in less than a year. It was unfathomable to think I'd be playing freshman basketball, or getting straight As, let alone being elected class president. I couldn't dream that I would be giving a speech to Harvard graduate students about my experience.

Last winter, I returned to Colorado. When I got onto the airplane, I started crying. I remembered the misery of being strapped to a stretcher on the med flight to Boston and crying because of a combination of pain, confusion, and the desire to get off the plane. It all came back to me. Sitting on the plane going back to the place that I came home from in such a damaged state, now my tears were a mix of relief and gratitude.

I met with the ski patrol team who rescued me. My outcome would have been hauntingly different had these heroes not worked so quickly. I felt blessed to meet my saviors. All my thanks could not come close to expressing my appreciation.

I skied the trail where the accident happened. Knowing that any of those trees could have been the one I hit, I trembled as I skied past them. Moving slowly and cautiously, I told myself, *I can do this*. For three years, I thought about getting back on the slopes that had changed my life. Now, I had done it. I finally felt I had conquered my injury.

Two months later, I returned to Spaulding. I remembered the comfort and support, regaining strength in my body, and rewiring my brain. I remembered realizing that my determination would heal me.

Every day, I am grateful for the details I remember and even for the time I don't.

 PROMPT: Write a piece using your high school voice about something you felt gratitude for.

SECRET FIVE

Use Direct Quotes

I need to hear people speak directly. I want to know them first-hand. Quote them, and I have a sense of them. Paraphrase them, and I sort of get a hint. But actual words coming out of the mouths of your characters, or actual quotes from historic figures or published writings, increase my understanding and my relationship with them. That's how I stay gripped in your essay, which is what you want. You want me consistently engaged. You'll lose me if I don't feel connected. Direct quotes are my direct line into the voice of the piece.

My Passionate Mother

Kate Feiffer

A few years ago, a writer friend asked me if there was a specific book that I considered to be my literary Waterloo. Was there a book I had hoped to conquer but hadn't been able to? While I have long planned to have read Stendhal's *The Red and the Black* and Dickens's *Bleak House*, the book that immediately came to mind was short, breezy, and X-rated.

A Hot Property is a mere 171 pages and was written by my mother, Judy Feiffer. The book was published in 1973, when I was a shy nine-year-old figuring out how to handle my combative parents who had recently split up. *A Hot Property* was called "funny" and "raunchy" by a *New York Times* reviewer, who also noted that my mother had found new and inventive ways to write about sex.

"Mrs. Feiffer manages, even at this late date, to introduce a few new wrinkles into the subject. To genital, oral and anal variations, she has added nasal."

I didn't read this or any other review, nor did I ever crack open the book, when I was a child. I assumed my mother had written a novel about real estate — after all, the title was *A Hot Property* — until my high school boyfriend plucked it off the shelf one day and started reading select passages aloud. Passages like, "Ubango's nose was grinding deeper. It pushed upward like a mole burrowing toward the sun. A moist, mucus fluid drained down her leg."

After my father left, my mother was anxious about money. While my father was providing child support, she clearly found whatever settlement they had agreed to insufficient. It was the early 1970s, and Jacqueline Susann had seduced millions of readers with her bestselling books *Valley of the Dolls* and *The Love Machine*. My mother must have thought she could be the next Jacqueline Susann. After all, they were both smart Jewish-born beauties who had a way with words.

My mother had recently died when my friend asked me this question about my literary Waterloo. It was time. I was ready to read *A Hot Property*. I would approach the book with the under-standing that my mother had written it as a single woman trying to support herself and her daughter. There weren't many high-paying jobs for women in the 1970s, and she saw an opportunity to make some money. She wasn't trying to embarrass me; she wrote it be-cause she wanted to be independent and financially responsible.

By the time I got to page 15, I was screaming, "No! Mom, no!"

By page 15, readers have been introduced to a bookish high school girl named Esther who is eager to start experiencing life. Her father is a literary agent, and she has reached out to one of his clients, a frustrated novelist who hasn't received the acclaim he believes is his due. His wife is out of town, and he invites Esther over. He even tells her he'll pay for her taxi.

And then on page 15, "He pulled down her Fruit of the Loom underpants and turned her over." On page 15, "He burst into her like a grenade, and she screamed in panic and pain."

But wait. In the early 1970s men in certain places and professions could sleep with high school students with impunity. Woody Allen proved that with his film *Manhattan*, in which a young Mariel Hemingway, whose character in the film was going to the same high school I attended, is dating a forty-two-year-old comedy writer played by Woody Allen. And that film came out in 1979, six years after my mother's book was published. My mother was writing about the mores of her time. She wasn't endorsing; she was reflecting. Perhaps she was even skewering.

It's challenging to forgive or even sit comfortably with what we now judge as unconscionable behavior — even when it's fictional — by allowing for the context of a different time. As I continued reading, there were many more bouts of "No! Mom, no!" I wondered, *How could she have written this? What was she thinking? What was she doing?* But now, as I write this, I realize she was bravely chronicling, if not commenting on, how a certain set of self-involved literary lions behaved.

The book didn't become a bestseller, perhaps because of the squirm-worthy nose-orgasmy scene, perhaps because it was misunderstood, perhaps because it was something other than a conventional potboiler. She later tried again with her novel *Flame* and a young-adult novel titled *Love Crazy*, which was about two best friends who try to seduce each other's fathers. I read both those books when they were published. Neither was easy for me to stomach, but I got through them.

The final book my mother wrote was titled *My Passionate Mother*. It was about a woman who had two great lovers in her life, but because my mother liked to push boundaries, one of the woman's lovers also falls into the arms of (No! Mom, no!) her daughter.

My passionate mother, indeed.

My Take

Here are a few reasons why I think Kate Feiffer's piece is brilliant:

I love when words that have never been next to each other flow easily, are original, and sound great together. "Literary Waterloo." Love it!

The specific Stendhal and Dickens titles are great details. They also tell us a bit about the writer's intellect, taste, and maturity.

"Short, breezy, and X-rated" is a great trio of adjectives. Plus, "X-rated" is a buzzword.

I love the specificity of numbers in an essay: 171 pages, 1973, and nine years old. Numbers are details that help the reader feel and know as much as possible.

Immediately when we read "shy nine-year-old," we know the narrator is vulnerable, with fighting parents who have just split up — the worst thing for a kid.

What the humiliation must have been with that *Times* review! The quotes from it are titillating and compelling. Plus, they reveal that her mother is a writer of some repute. This is a perfect "show, don't tell."

The real estate line is funny, and she places it in the perfect position.

The word "plucked" is perfect — the sound's resemblance to "f**ked," the action of what plucking is. You can visualize the boy-friend, not perusing the bookshelves, but going right for it.

The quote from the book is hysterical. The opposite of titillating and suggestive. It's repulsive and funny at the same time.

Then comes the explanation and compassion and understanding of what her mother was going through. So the author has shifted into her grown-up voice with the wisdom of retrospection. Until page 15. And here she cracks me up again with "No! Mom, no!"

With the quote of "He burst into her..." we are mortified along with the narrator until "But wait." And then she places it in cultural context and goes back to explaining and justifying what her mother had done. Men have been doing this forever. So our writer, who has vacillated between embarrassment and pride (taking us with her on the roller-coaster ride), is beginning to see her mother as a hero, a feminist forging new paths for women.

More understanding, more books, more attempts at breaking boundaries, more compassion for her mother. And more humor with "No! Mom, no." They work because she doesn't overdo it and because they are placed exactly right.

And then her last line is total forgiveness and redemption.

 PROMPT: Write an embarrassing mother story (yours).

If You Can't Say Anything Nice, Write a One-Star Review

Jane Lancellotti

"THIS BOOK SUCKED!" "Vastly overrated!" "Boring!" "Tedious!" "Waste of time!" "Just shoot me!" They were all screaming at him — I mean at my friend, whom I'll call Howard, who got great reviews in *The New York Times* and *The Washington Post* for his latest novel but who couldn't stop the shouting from internet reviewers, whose inspirational and cheerfully inventive names all sounded like JerkWadJunior, EffYou69, and DarthReader. The whole negativity thing was getting to him, big-time.

"Have no fear," I told Howard. I'd monitor the internet. I'd take time off from my one, singular guilty pleasure in watching footage of celebrities leaving restaurants on TMZ.com and check his reviews instead. It'd be fun. I'd spare him the screaming memies, I said. Let him know if the snoozers and slammers lived up to their names. That was the plan, anyway, until on my watch Howard got his first one-star review, and I got mad. I got so mad

I scrolled obsessively through reader reviews of literary master-pieces that have stood the test of time. What did the Howie-haters have to say about *Jane Eyre* and *Pride and Prejudice* or any of the ones you wish you could read for the first time? God help me, I opened the door onto those reviews the way you might peer into the refrigerator after midnight to see what's lurking behind the cheese. With some appetite but not expecting much, I began with reviews of *Pride and Prejudice* because who, after all, would take on Jane Austen?

Answer: forty tremendously bored and really, really disap-pointed readers.

"I felt the same annoyance as when sitting next to a loud-mouthed idiot in a train," wrote one of *Pride and Prejudice*. "Not worth reading," another whined, because "the story line is boring" and "the characters are not well developed." Hold your ponies: Were we talking about the same Austen, the quintessential novelist of social manners, the genial satirist?

I called Howard.

"How bad is it?" he asked.

"Let me put things in perspective," I said and read him a thought-provoking review of Shakespeare. "Nothing earth-shattering on jealousy [*sic*]" in *Othello*. I skipped through the centu-ries to William Gaddis, who uses "so much adjective [*sic*]" in *The Recognitions* and is "so full of himself" as to be "not worth reading."

"Point taken," he said. "You can stop now."

But I couldn't. George Eliot, Edith Wharton, Willa Cather — no author dodged readers who were indifferent to literary mas-terpieces and offered such evaluations as this one of *My Ántonia*: "I've seen trash on the curb with more plot than this." Meanwhile, Howard received a one-star along the lines of "not worth the paper it was written on."

"The highest Criticism," Oscar Wilde wrote in his famous essay "The Critic as Artist," "is more creative than creation."

What he meant, of course, is that the riches of the imagination are as crucial in judging art as they are in creating it. Notice how the godlike capital *C* for *Criticism* is working here. How it makes you wish that Wilde himself could show up next to the reviewer's desktop and cover the whole darn keyboard with his paisley cravat to prevent the cynic from posting that he would rather scoop out an eye with a rusty spoon than read *Great Expectations*.

Through the ages, there have been major thinkers, such as Matthew Arnold, whose fluency and insight elevated the ways in which we talk about art. Only now, instead of Arnold of Great Britain, we have Arnie from Massapequa, who misguidedly equates *Jane Eyre* with "another of those cheesey [*sic*] love novels written by Danielle Steel."

"It's only a lack of education," Howie said of the Arnies. Or a kind of literary autism in which a reader tries to connect with the classics and can't. It wasn't until I overheard a classroom of MFA writing students reveal to their professor that they were more influenced by the opinions of amateur online reviewers than by those written by acknowledged pros that I realized how truly and righteously screwed we are when people with screen names as ludicrous as old CB handles — Buzbo, ChaCha, and Good-Buddy — let you know before you buy *To Kill a Mockingbird* that "it sucked, just like any other book."

The internet has always held a special place in its big bloggy heart for the cranky and disgruntled. The speed and anonymity of the Web make it irresistible to the one-star reviewer, in much the same way that a blank wall and a can of black spray paint are irresistible to a pissed-off adolescent. The Web is threaded with the complaints and disparagements of people who feel compelled to remark on the "timidity" of steak sauce or to cast a vote on whether Cindy Crawford has (a) good genes or (b) good docs or (c) both. And while it's true that there are also thoughtful, well-considered, well-written comments online, there may never have been a meaner, less inhibited group of haters than one-star book reviewers. Consider the reviewer who would "rather have a coffee enema" than read *To the Lighthouse*; another who would "rather slit [his] wrists than read one more page" of *Madame Bovary*; and another who writes of *Wuthering Heights*: "Quick! Gouge out my eyes!!!" Why must readers link violence, enemas, blood, and blinding with the act of reading?

One way to climb inside the mind of the one-star reviewer is to take him up on his invitation to have a look at his other reviews. What else is a guy from Los Angeles ripping apart besides Doctorow's *Ragtime*? Why, it's packing tape, a product he hails with five stars because he can rip it apart with his fingers. Or his canines. And what about the singularly unappeasable critic who not only is "done with" Hemingway after reading *The Sun Also Rises* but also hated the lip-piercing set by GlitZ JewelZ, complained about the Velvet Kitten Satin Booty, and couldn't stomach a long curly wig, which, "despite styling, remains a bit lifeless." Oh, yeah. She also condemns Hemingway's prose for remaining "a bit lifeless." Wigs and art — can they really be the same? Has online reviewing become the nicest possible way to kill time while on hold with the Better Business Bureau?

"It all stems from the same thing," says Sherry Turkle in her book *Alone Together: Why We Expect More from Technology and Less from Each Other* (a 305-page work that received a one-star for being 299 pages too long). "When we are face to face, we are inhibited from aggression by the presence of another face, another person. We're aware that we're with a human being." That got me wondering: What if another of those anonymous reviewers found herself face-to-face with National Book Award winner Louise Erdrich? Would the reviewer have accused Erdrich of being a weird older woman writing a smutty page-turner from the perspective of a thirteen-year-old boy?

A person venting gratuitous irritation by giving a one-star rating to Toni Morrison for her "poorly constructed" novel *Sula* finds confirmation in the echoes of fellow one-star commentators that come in a barrage of "I totally agree!" and "Your [*sic*] so right," fulfilling the quest for at least one fellow negative to be listening and agreeing. The reviewer who never finished reading *Pride and Prejudice* but disparaged the novel anyway finds a chorus of agreeers. "Plot?? What plot??" (one question mark being insufficient for her disdain). Same for the guy who couldn't follow the story of the impotent Jake Barnes in *The Sun Also Rises* but reviewed the book, without a hint of wit or irony, under a pseudonym inspired by male genitalia. "This is Ernest Hemingway????" he grumbles. "What is the point???"

Who are these people? Are they online versions of the bully who kicks over bicycles? Or the kid who gets his bicycle kicked over? Or are they, more likely, past-hopeful writers whose thwarted ambitions propelled a spite-filled review of Philip Roth? Roth is blamed for being "established" and "no longer bound to be at his very best, because the work will be published one way or another." One Roth detractor hints that if she were to write a novel, she would deliver a far better result than *American Pastoral*.

My pal Howard waxed poetic. "What we have," he noted, "is a subculture of literary vandals who have replaced the light of intellect with the ruinous glow of a single emoji star from which no author can hide."

If there's one thing the internet has taught us, it's that it reflects all of society: those interested in a true exchange of ideas and those who relish the click-based titillation of a nasty comment directed at the immortals. "Shakespeare is s*** y duz every1 think he iz so gr8 like wat did he evr do 4 man kind." Authors beware.

 PROMPT: Write a nice review of your (potential) book.

Out of the Mouths of Babes

Nancy Slonim Aronie

Remember George W. Bush's No Child Left Behind Act?

It was a lofty idea that didn't work then, and with one in six American children living below the poverty line today, it's obvious that more than 11 million children have been left behind.

A month ago, I vacationed in Naples, Florida, and I met six-year-old Jack in the pool where I was staying.

He said, "I bet you can't guess my birthday."

"December 20th," I said.

"Nooooooo," he practically screamed with delight.

"Um," I pretended to think, "July 9th?"

"Nooooo," he yelled even more enthusiastically.

"April 7th?" I asked.

This time he was almost apoplectic in his joy when he sang "nooooooo." And then he said, "Do you give up?"

And I said, "Yup."

And then with this grave, serious look on his face, he said, "You should never give up."

Wow, I thought. *The kid is six? And he just said 'you should never give up'???* I said, "That's profound, Jack. That's really cool that you know that."

He continued, "I had a little meltdown when we first got here yesterday."

I said, "What happened?"

He said, "Well, I had new goggles, and they broke immediately."

By this time, the mom had floated over to the shallow end where Jack and I were talking. She said, "And what do we do when we are frustrated, Jack?"

He said, "We switch our attitude to gratitude."

"And what else, Jack?"

He said, "Deep breaths, deep breaths."

Now I'm blown away. And I want a do-over raising my poor kids.

I said, "Your boy is very special. I mean, all of our kids are, but this little guy…wow."

She said, "Well, he goes to a private school, and they have mindfulness training. They actually meditate each morning."

Now I'm gobsmacked. A six-year-old is meditating? He's learning coping skills for stress? Are you kidding me? It thrills me that he is getting the best of the best.

But then it breaks my heart that every kid isn't getting the best of the best.

What kind of world are we living in that kids are hungry? And how can you learn if you're hungry? How can you concentrate if you haven't eaten? How can you function if you are hungry? When my stomach has even an inclination to growl, I get to feed it immediately.

How does it feel to be the mother of a hungry child? How do Bush and all the other politicians before and since who are letting this happen feel knowing about all the children that got left behind?

How do I feel? Horrible. Just heartbreakingly horrible.

There are so many injustices right now. It's overwhelming and frustrating.

I don't have answers or solutions. I only have outrage.

I'll take a page from Jack's playbook.

Deep breaths. Deep breaths.

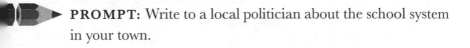

PROMPT: Write to a local politician about the school system in your town.

"What a Waste to Train a Woman as a Doctor," He Said

Lissa Rankin

I'd been quaking in my boots as I anticipated telling the medical director of my hospital that I was resigning from practicing as an

OB-GYN in the hospital — for good, at the ripe old age of thirty-seven. I had enough self-doubt already.

I didn't know about Internal Family Systems yet, so I didn't know how to reckon with the scared, mean inner critic voices in my head that were screaming, *What the actual f**k are you doing? You spent twelve years and racked up $200,000 in school debt learning to be an OB-GYN! You sacrificed your entire twenties while all your friends were off having a life, earning money, getting married, having babies, and backpacking Europe so you could help others heal, have a stable career, enjoy a meaningful job. You have a newborn baby whose father has never been employed the whole time you've been together — and you have no other legitimate means of earning an income. You are the most irresponsible mother, partner, doctor, human being on this earth if you walk out of this hospital!*

I didn't particularly need to hear what the medical director thought about my scary decision, but I had to tell him. It didn't particularly help when I approached him in the dark mahogany doctor's lounge where pretty Latinx girls in short-skirted waitress costumes were serving the male doctors (but never us lady doctors), and, without missing a beat, he responded flatly to my news with, "What a waste to train a woman as a doctor."

He went off on a rant about how you have to train two men to equal one woman in medicine, since we're all so lazy and inclined to quit the profession when we can't hack the pressure, or when we become mothers who want to breastfeed our babies or feel entitled to do stupid, weak things, like sleep at night. He kept going, talking about how women were such inferior doctors and universities shouldn't bother to give us the privilege of an education if we were going to shirk our duties to society and neglect the people who needed us once we had the skills necessary to save lives because we cared about things like family life and our own mental or physical health. It left me frozen and silenced.

I had graduated second in my class in medical school, just behind a woman who was a nurse first and a better doctor than me and deserved to be valedictorian. I wondered if she was struggling too. Or maybe she was just stronger and more capable of being like men expect women to be in medicine, which is how men expect men to be in medicine, which is to devalue everything but medicine, including your own family and your own health.

As his angry, corrosive voice ripped into me, I felt myself falling into a pit I knew well — the sinkhole of shame. His voice took on a rushing sound, like I was in a tunnel, and he was very far away. My visual field started narrowing, and I wondered if I was about to black out. I prayed to a God I was no longer sure I believed in, just in case there was any way divine intervention might prevent me from the humiliation of passing out in front of the medical director who was berating me.

I guess I dissociated, because I have total amnesia about what happened next, other than hearing rumors from others who had been there that his rant had been misogynistic and insulting enough to upset others and that someone had apparently told him off on my behalf.

He hadn't asked me why I was leaving, even though, as medical director, he really should have known that I was jumping ship because my new boss was insisting I perform unethical, medical malpractice–worthy C-sections on undocumented Mexican women who were migrant workers in the farm fields, without even bringing in a translator or getting their consent. Someone should have told him my boss and his partner were raking in the dough, taking advantage of innocent patients who didn't have enough power to say no, fight for their rights, or challenge authority.

He probably wouldn't have cared anyway, but if I hadn't frozen, maybe I could have told him that I'd refused to do a C-section on a woman with twins whose babies were too premature — when there was zero medical indication to deliver those babies early — and when I'd said no to my boss because it would have been wrong for me to endanger those babies by saying yes, I'd been told "It's our way or the highway."

When my physician colleague did the C-section because I refused, those preemies wound up sick in the NICU — and it was all his fault. The doctor who did the C-section came to me crying after he'd heard I'd chosen the highway instead of agreeing to do what he too knew was wrong in order to keep his paycheck. He said he wished he'd been brave enough to say no like I did, but that he was scared of losing his job. I told him I was scared of losing mine too, but I could not live with more preventable wreckage on my hands. I'd rather be broke.

He said his wife would kill him if he lost his job. I said my husband probably wouldn't be too happy with me either.

But I still chose the highway.

I'd already left one hospital where I suffered moral injury so severe that I became sick and suicidal. I'd escaped to this one, hoping things would be better, but they were worse.

I heard through the grapevine years later that my boss's medical license had been revoked — thank Goddess. But I always wondered if there was any accountability for that medical director whose name I no longer remember (funny how dissociation can wipe the memory slate that clean). I never found out how those babies or those Mexican mothers fared after I left. Parts of me regret not calling an investigative reporter and blowing the whistle or reporting my bosses to the medical board when I left. But I was too traumatized. I spent the next two years writing my stories privately. And then one day, I started telling my stories publicly and realized I could be a different kind of doctor, not an utter waste like that medical director wrote me off as, but as a doctor of doctors and a voice for the voiceless.

 PROMPT: Write about a time you felt you were morally injured.

How I Met Her

Glenn Bergenfield

I always thought Lloyd was a Jewish name, like Irv or Sol. Maybe a nickname for Lawrence? In those days I assessed everything as "Good for the Jews" / "Not Good for the Jews." Now I see that this stance — of course! — does not embrace everything one should consider as one lives this puzzling and sometimes beautiful life. In fact, this binary — handed down from my father and his father and a thousand generations of chanting, weeping, plucky Jews — obscured and complicated as much as it uncovered. It isn't right to go around asking Christians if they would hide you or not; it annoys them and creates the very response feared: "Let's not hide him — he's so needy!"

Lloyd is a Welsh name, spelled Llwyd in its original form, and David Lloyd George, the only Welshman to be British prime minister, is probably the most famous holder of that name. Now, there is the rapper Lloyd, Lloyd Taco Factory, and Lloyd the Green Ninja Legos character. A Hasidic website advises that the Hebrew name for Lloyd is Adar. No explanation is given as to why this is so.

Lloyd has no Jewish root.

And Lloyd's of London, come to find out, is not about the Jews either.

In 1985 I was a young lawyer sent to London to take a two-day deposition of who I thought was the "underwriter of Lloyd's of London." It started with this:

Q: So, you are the underwriter at Lloyd's of London?
A: No.
Q: Well, that's who I asked for.
A: Yes.
Q: Do you know where he is?
A: No.

Q: Do you work for Lloyd's of London?

A: Not really, no.

Q: Aren't we sitting in the Lloyd's building?

A: Yes.

Q: Do you work in this building?

A: Yes.

Q: Didn't a lawyer — er, solicitor Spencer — set up this deposition with you as "the underwriter for Lloyd's?"

A: Yes.

Q: But you are not "the underwriter of Lloyd's of London."

A: No.

He fixed me with a placid and yet very cold look. It seemed I amused him. I narrowed my eyes and leaned forward, trying to evoke threat to cover my confusion, my near fright at how lost I was.

"Lloyd's of London," he said with a gentleman's contempt, "is a rubric." And for him, that was that, clearing up the Yank's nonsense.

Huh? A rubric? Wasn't that some Church of England word? Some liturgical something offered just before the eunuch choir sings their high-pitched hymns to the queen?

I didn't ask any good questions. It was only seven hours of ineptitude, but it seemed much longer. I didn't understand what Lloyd's was or how it worked. It seemed that certain English families agreed by "treaties" to share the risk of, among other things in this world, a fire to a commercial building in Hackensack, New Jersey. Not only couldn't I be told those names, but there was also no insurance policy issued, no file, no notes of anything. There was insurance, true enough, but the policy that had not been issued by the people I would never meet, and the notes that may not have been created, all precluded coverage for the Hackensack fire and the water damage and vandalism that followed.

Clear, Yank?

I was a stranger, a naïf, a Brooklyn Jew in King Arthur's Court. Lloyd's was not good for the Jews; but it wasn't bad for the Jews either. The binary was breaking down under the weight of this puzzling culture, this man's utter contempt for me. Lloyd's of London was British. That is, secretive, smug, and amused — with family ties and coats of arms and a shameful history (insuring ships carrying slaves and the massive theft from India) that was seen as glorious.

It was a secret why the fire claim was denied — unless it was just that I was an ignorant, contemptible lawyer, powerless to do anything about it.

At the end of the day, I took a bus back through London to my hotel, feeling defeated and questioning my choice of careers. I was a lawyer — true — just not a good lawyer. Was there room in the profession for someone like me, with no particular talent?

I was dozing on the bus, lulled and then jolted awake, again and again, by exhaustion and my anxious sense of failure. One more day of his contempt and my ineptitude, and then home.

Then I saw a young guy get on the bus. He had a black leather jacket and, as he soon revealed, a knife. He was flicking it open and closed. There was a poster on this bus, and it said: "A real man will carry his Nan's shopping, not a knife. Grow up!"

Contempt didn't work on everyone.

He went up to people and, while flicking the knife, said, "Fare, please!" like a conductor might do. "Fare, please" to the terrified adults and schoolkids on the bus, "Fare, please" in his demonic way. The accent had lost its charm for me seven hours earlier — and now this.

Understandably, everyone was handing over some money to this thief. Better to lose a few quid than get stabbed. The two cultures had this in common.

There were three Catholic schoolgirls, in uniforms, and he

didn't spare them. Two forked over their schoolkid fares. Then he turned to the third one, flicked his knife, and said with a sneer, "Fare, please."

She was very thin, as tall as he was, with short blondish hair, high cheekbones, schoolbooks in her right arm, a purse over her left shoulder. She fixed him with a placid and yet very cold look — the same one I'd seen all day at what might have been Lloyd's of London — and, after a dramatic pause, she said: "I'm not giving you my fare, you wanker." Then she bumped him, actually shoved him out of her way and headed for the middle door to get off. The robber, the "twocker," looked around at all of us, more stunned than we were. "Did you see that?" he seemed to be saying. He put his knife away, got off the bus, and went the opposite way — didn't want to run into that schoolgirl again.

Give up the life, mate. You don't have what it takes!

I watched her walk down the block — such very long legs — turn the corner and disappear.

I felt great — "chuffed, rosy about the gills," as I came to describe it, though that was years later, once I'd learned more colorful Britishisms.

I could see that the problem I had with Lloyd was not my problem but his. Or theirs, or whatever it was. It was an insurance company with no policy, no notes, no file. Let this guy tell a New Jersey jury that it or he or someone was a "rubric" and that this was part of the reason why they didn't have to pay for the building that burned down in town, about a block from the courthouse in Hackensack.

The "underwriter" was the wanker, not me. I was the Catholic schoolgirl!

Tomorrow I was going to bump him and then go home. And he could look at my ass as I turned and walked out of Lloyd's.

The next day it all went perfectly. His contempt for me was useless to him this time. It was comical, almost laugh-out-loud funny. OK, OK, you're a rubric! I get it, Lloyd!

I was out of there in two hours.

I went to the Rivoli Bar at the Ritz. There was a picture of Charlie Chaplin. In *The Great Dictator* he'd made fun of Hitler! Not a guy like Hitler, not *a* Hitler, but Hitler. Called him Adenoid Hynkel. And had him look like "unnamed Jewish barber." Chaplin was unafraid of Hitler before England was unafraid of Hitler. Except Churchill. He wasn't afraid of Hitler either. He favored the Ritz as well, and his picture was there too. And I thought of that schoolgirl, what she'd done and how she was unafraid. She was a lot like Churchill, I thought, in my glorious drunken joy. Except how she looked as she walked away. Churchill had a huge ass. I knew it was wrong, even then in the '80s, to think of a school-girl that way. She was maybe fifteen. But a writer's only duty is to truth. And that's what I was thinking about: Charlie Chaplin, Hitler, Churchill, and those long, beautiful legs.

Twelve years later I was in London again — to see Wimble-don, sure — but also to escape the mess I'd made of my life. My unhappy, depressed, unfaithful wife. My wild kids. My sad parents and friends who watched the train head toward the bridge that was out, powerless to do anything but watch.

I was taking the overground from London to Wimbledon, with a pretty good Centre Court seat in my pocket. It was hot and the train was hot. Like a lot of things at that time, it seemed like a long slog.

And then I saw a beautiful woman just the other side of the train car, only three or four feet away. Was it, perhaps...? She was in a short skirt, and in that very careful, thoughtful way that my gender does this, I took a gander at her legs.

Now, legs are, allegedly, not distinct and particular like faces. They don't exude pheromones, as far as science can tell us. Foren-sic pathologists identify Jane Does by their teeth, not by their legs.

Still, this was excellent proof. And then I looked up at her as the train pulled into the stop. Wimbledon. She was getting off too. I walked over to her as she was getting off. "It was you, that time, wasn't it?" I blurted out. She fixed me with that placid but cold stare — it was definitely her! And then her face softened, just a tiny bit, into a face the guy with the knife had not seen.

"You told the guy with the knife — the wanker — that he couldn't have your bus money. That was fantastic, awesome."

She stood there and looked into my eyes, considering me. "What are you," she said, a tiny smile forming, "some kind of spy?"

And those were the first words Sarah said to me.

 PROMPT: Write about a time someone in authority made you feel small.

Juneteenth Is a Big Fat Lie

Abigail McGrath

This week President Biden made Juneteenth an official national holiday. That means you get the day off from work, the post offices are closed, and so are the schools.

It means that it is a day for celebration, joy, festivities all over the United States.

This should be good news. The only occasion/event that I know of that has cheerfulness associated with the color black is Black Friday.

So why am I (a predominantly Black person) not jumping up and down for joy?

Because Juneteenth is a big fat lie. Juneteenth is about keeping people enslaved for two and a half years after they were freed. Juneteenth is about the government lying to people so that the wealthy could have free labor. Tell me, where is the joy in that? It is like celebrating all the broken treaties that the US made with the Native Americans.

OK, the folks in Galveston, Texas, should be happy, because

had things gone the other way, they might still be enslaved. Texans could be like the Japanese soldiers in World War II who survived on small islands and didn't know the war was over for another twenty-five years. I don't see the Japanese having marching bands for that.

OK, so it's June 19, 1865. The legislature of Galveston, Texas, which is the westernmost area in the Union at that time, gives up the charade. Two thousand federal troops, who were mostly Black, arrived in the last unoccupied Confederate state to tell the slaves that the Emancipation Proclamation was signed in 1863, and that they were free.

President Abraham Lincoln had outlawed slavery two years prior, but there was a glitch in the teletype machine, and we're just now finding out. Oh, and look, we're a tad tardy getting the crops out — why don't we wait until next year in 1866 to celebrate? What's another six months?

It's just a small technicality here. You have been free for over two years. Back pay? I don't think so. Forty acres and a mule? Oh dear, that's all been given out. But you are free, free as a bird to do anything you want as long as you don't want what the white people won't give you.

General Gordon Granger, who led the Union troops, made a big speech. In it he said:

> The people of Texas are informed that in accordance with a proclamation from the Executive of the United States, all slaves are free. This involves an absolute equality of personal rights and property rights between former mas-ters and slaves, and the connection heretofore existing between them becomes that between employer and hired labor. The freedmen are advised to remain quietly at their present homes and work for wages.
>
> They are informed that they will not be allowed to

collect at military posts, and that they will not be supported in idleness either there or elsewhere.

Idleness? Remain home and hope "Ole Massa" is going to give them wages?

Many, many slaves did not remain quietly at their present homes. They headed out to their families, their real homes. Entire plantations were left empty with only white people to work them.

Felix Haywood, a North Carolina–born Texan, rejoiced in the news, which he heard in 1865. He knew it was a double-edged sword.

Soldiers, all of a sudden, was everywhere — coming in bunches, crossing and walking and riding. Everyone was a-singing. We was all walking on golden clouds. Hallelujah!…Nobody took our homes away, but right off, colored folks started on the move. They seemed to want to get closer to freedom, so they'd know what it was — like it was was a place or a city.…

We knowed freedom was on us, but we didn't know what was to come with it. We thought we was going to get rich like the white folks. We thought we was going to be richer than the white folks, 'cause we was stronger and knowed how to work, and the whites didn't, and they didn't have us to work for them anymore. But it didn't turn out that way. We soon found out that freedom could make folks proud, but it didn't make 'em rich.

It also made the white people angry. Wouldn't you be angry if something you'd paid good money for up and walked away, and left you and your entitled family to toil in the fields?

Confederate soldiers put on their newly doffed uniforms and began a campaign of intimidation, murder, and lynching that soothed their wounds of losing the war. Taking it out on the unarmed made them feel more in control of themselves, and they had the power of the uniform to make their horrific actions seem valid.

The resiliency of Black people is mind-boggling. That a race would not turn bitter, would not seek revenge under those circumstances, proves their superiority in adjusting to cataclysmic situations. Instead of harsh, hostile reactions to the duplicity, we choose to see the half-full glass and celebrate the goodness with parades, picnics, and parties. Nothing good can come from harboring evil in your heart.

I often think that the true losers of the agony of slavery are the white people. They were robbed of feeling empathy. They lost their sense of humanity and became obsessed with covering up their sins, whitewashing the facts so that they didn't have to endure the pain of guilt. So that they didn't have to feel the residual effects of their ancestors and the silent advantages they were given at birth.

To this day, whenever Black people try to crawl out of the pit that white supremacy has dug for them, they are labeled "socialists" or "thugs" or "anti-American." Who is more American than the African American? Who keeps trying to make the country better while getting kicked in the teeth?

James Baldwin said, "American history is longer, larger, more various, more beautiful, and more terrible than anything anyone has ever said about it."

So now we have a national holiday in which we do as Johnny Mercer says:

We gotta accentuate the positive
Eliminate the negative
Latch on to the affirmative
Don't mess with Mister In-Between

You've got to spread joy up to the maximum
Bring gloom down to the minimum

Have faith or pandemonium
Liable to walk upon the scene

Yeah, I get it. I get why we celebrate it. I don't get why we don't celebrate the actual Emancipation Proclamation, but it's better to be a cheerful soul than a dystopian.

 PROMPT: Write a piece about a time you were a cheerful soul instead of what you could have been: an angry dystopian.

Incorporate the Three-Part Narrative

*I*n school I always hated having to do outlines, and I hated the word *structure*. In my ADHD mind, I was probably just rebelling against organization, which still is my downfall.

But at least I'm not getting a B minus and a note at the end of my composition saying, "Nancy, your writing is quite good, but you really have to structure your work in a more cohesive way." And on and on the red squiggles went.

Now I am a convert. You really need a structure. And with the personal narrative, you need a beginning (an introduction), a body (the story), and a conclusion (the end). Each of these serves a specific purpose:

- The intro sets the stage, gives context and background information, and introduces the theme (oy, another word I hated but since have made my peace with) or main topic of the essay. And don't forget: Here's where you must capture your reader's attention.
- The body is where the essay unfolds and the main points are developed.
- The conclusion is where you summarize. You write the significance of the story and provide (my favorite) clo-sure — so satisfying — or in some cases, a tantalizing cliff-hanger

Mind you, as Jean-Luc Godard said about his films, all stories need a beginning, middle, and end — "but not necessarily in that order." In other words, the beginning of your essay doesn't have to be the beginning of your story. Sometimes the strongest beginnings put the reader into the middle of the action. So feel free to experiment with nonlinear timelines within the overall three-part structure.

Just a Dumb Idea

John Abrams

In 1890 my grandfather's mother died as he was born in Kyiv, Ukraine. A neighborhood family who had just lost a baby offered to raise him. Soon his father left for America to seek new opportunity, and in 1899 he arranged passage for his son on a ship bound for New York. The vessel arrived on New Year's Eve of 1899 — the turning of the century. The vibrant capital of New World commerce was decked out and lit up. As the ship edged into the harbor, nine-year-old Morris Abrams was perched in the bow, spellbound by the spectacle before him. Fireworks blazed across the night sky and touched his heart. It was like a greeting just for him. He instantly fell in love with America. The flames of this lifelong passion were never doused until he died weeks before his hundredth birthday.

In his early teens, Morris went to work for a hardware merchant named Lemkin on Center Street in lower Manhattan and helped build the business. When Lemkin, nearing retirement, refused Morris a partnership and prepared to pass the business on to his own son, my grandfather decided it was time to set up shop on his own. Just down the street, at 196 Center, Morris Abrams Inc. was established in 1922 to supply hardware, tools, machinery, and equipment to manufacturers, retailers, and contractors. They weathered two world wars and the Great Depression, thrived, and by 1950 the payroll had swelled to 110 employees.

The business moved to larger quarters at 90 Hudson Street, a dignified seven-story building that occupied most of a city block and was capped by eighteen great arched windows on the top floor. The 569-page Morris Abrams Inc. clothbound catalog from 1955 is black with embossed red-and-white lettering. On page 195, one of the many toolboxes illustrated is the Union Super Steel Cantilever tool chest, listed at $5.60. This is the one I'd see beside my grandfather's desk when my father dropped me off at his office on visits from our home in San Francisco. My grandfather would hand me the new toolbox and tell me, "Explore the stockrooms, fill it up, have fun, and behave yourself."

I did all that, hauled the toolbox onto the DC-7 for the long flight home, and had lost pretty much everything in it by the time we returned two years later for the next round of this ritual.

None of my grandfather's three children was interested in the business. Their father's message about the value of education carried them to varied fields of interest. Skipping a generation, however, my grandfather's love for tools and the things they can make somehow passed on to me. His optimism too.

My father, a physician and fierce intellectual, was disappointed when I took an entirely different path from his. When I started college in 1967, the Vietnam War was raging and America's youth were outraged. On a sunny October day, I joined one hundred thousand others at the Lincoln Memorial for the largest antiwar protest to date and marched on to the Pentagon, which was ringed with soldiers bearing rifles. We put flowers in the barrels. Occasionally a soldier would throw down his rifle and join the cheering crowd.

Meanwhile, the back-to-the-land movement was picking up steam as young people moved to rural America to attempt to learn the skills of self-sufficiency and invent a different future from the one we were raised to. I never finished college because that summons drew me in, hook, line, and sinker. This migration became my higher education. Stewart Brand's *Whole Earth Catalog* was my primary textbook. In its pages, and in the rural outbacks of

Vermont, Northern California, Oregon, and British Columbia, I inadvertently found a path to a fulfilling career that began by making crude houses and fixing up dilapidated ones. In those days I was more at home in America's agrarian past than in mainstream society's present.

This was rough for my dad. Although he admired my independence and initiative, he felt that I had turned my back on everything he held dear. Our relationship, while full of mutual love and respect, was also characterized by intense disagreement and conflict that lasted long after we'd both grown weary of it. I'd pretty much had it with his judgmental attitude, and I'm sure he'd had it with my inappropriately strident responses. After a particularly difficult year in the '90s, I wrote to him on Father's Day.

I said, "You are in your seventies. We have only so much time left. Maybe ten years, maybe fifteen, maybe more. I have a dumb idea that I want to share with you. How about this: What if, for the rest of our lives, until the day you die, we toss all conflict aside and celebrate each other, all the time? All…the…time. How about that?"

My brief message inspired a breathtaking response. He wrote eloquently about our lives, and at the end, he said, "I'm in. Let's do it." He was in, with the full complement of his unshakable optimism. And we did it — not just did it, but *really* did it — for the rest of his days.

(Except once, in 2005, after a very rare mild disagreement instigated by me, he bluntly reminded me, "Hey, you're not holding up your end of the bargain." We both laughed, and that was the end of it.)

My father lived to ninety-five, and we both cherished our reconciliation for all those years.

Sometimes an unlikely idea, expressed, can animate tectonic shifts. I think my grandfather's experience on the bow of that ship at the turning of the century and the sunny outlook that resulted and came to define his life were responsible for the latent qualities in my father and me that allowed us to open our minds, turn the tide, and change each other's lives. Pure dumb luck.

I miss them both.

My Take

The beginning of this three-part narrative sets up the story with two high-energy details: the date and the city, 1890 and Kyiv.

"Decked out and lit up." Listen to the rhythm of those two phrases. And when I say "listen," I mean "listen." That means you have to read them *out loud*!

Getting Morris's name and age right up front helps the reader feel informed and become engaged with the narrative.

"Ship," "spellbound," "spectacle," "sky" — nice alliteration.

Knowing the author's grandfather fell in love with America sets up his relationship with his new life and what's to come, and learning he lived to be almost one hundred makes us interested in the whole middle section of his long life.

There is a universality to the boss leaving the business to his son instead of to his devoted employee, and here's where the grandfather's character is developed. He will either sink or swim. He swims, and since we already love the nine-year old, we are cheering Morris on. The specific numbers — the years 1922 and 1950, the 110 employees, and the addresses 196 Center and 90 Hudson Street — jump into our consciousness and enrich the piece.

Now Morris has his own establishment. The reader is feeling hopeful and proud of what this "kid" has accomplished. Practically no one survives two wars, and we know how many businesses died during the Depression. So he's becoming a hero.

The description of the building is powerful: seven stories, arched windows. And a full city block! Only in America (*Then, not now*, we may be thinking).

The details about the catalog — the pages, the colors, and the embossing — add literal color and depth.

Hearing the grandfather tell the narrator to go explore, with all that freedom, gives us a sense of what a healthy, loving relationship they had. And you get a sense of what shaped the writer and his future: his love for tools and — this is the big one — his optimism.

Now part two: The description of the author's father as a "fierce intellectual" and a physician who is disappointed in his son's life choices marks the beginning of the conflict.

Our writer explains what is going on in the world and how he, like so many who were college age during the Vietnam War, was affected and changed. The echo in "raging" and "outraged" is beautiful.

The detail of "Occasionally a soldier would throw down his rifle and join the cheering crowd" adds a layer I don't think I knew happened. And I love hearing that. (See how good writing makes you think you're hearing and not reading?)

The rebellion of kids who choose a different path from their parents and the rebellion of the back-to-the-land movement is one focus of the story. And this is who this writer grew up to be! This is where this writer went. And when the writer is authentic and clear and not trying to sound like a "writer," we will follow him anywhere. Here is where the narrator shows us his process of evolving into who he ultimately (in part three) becomes.

Now the conflict: a very universal one between father and son, about the writer's choices and the father's dreams.

The writer shows accountability by acknowledging his own shortcomings and not just blaming and being judgmental about his father's reaction to him, which makes us relate to and admire this character. After all, it would have been easy to just put his father down and act as if he were an innocent party being unsupported. Using love and respect, he makes us hopeful for a good outcome. But we're still concerned as well.

Part three begins with that letter and what he calls his "dumb idea." This is the map! How do we handle trying to be our authentic selves and get what we want and not hurt the ones we love?

Twenty years of therapy couldn't have done better than that letter. And I don't know about you, but when his father said, "I'm in," I cried.

"Sometimes an unlikely idea, expressed, can animate tectonic shifts." Yes! "Tectonic" is the perfect word! Because it's true.

Coming back to the grandfather at the end is so satisfying for the reader. Always, if you can, circle back to your beginning. The closure is an exhale.

And we all know by now how I'm in love with threes, like this one: "open our minds, turn the tide, and change each other's lives." "Open," "turn," and "change."

Great writing, great structure for a three-piece narrative.

 PROMPT: Write about an actual reconciliation or an imagined one.

Bellowing the Truth

DeDe Lahman

I can't think of anything I didn't tell because there's something about the truth that makes me stand in total candor, like it's a hot shower in an arctic snow and I bathe in the liberation of the world and my thoughts joining together in loud song as declaration of everything I know to be true. Like an odd old uncle with bad teeth and gummy coin purses, I march around the city dodging puddles of pee, smeared sidewalk shit, and crazy-dressed people, hearing their thoughts, muzzling my mouth so that wild spiders don't fly out unsolicited, saying what you should do, how you should walk, where you should talk with that loud conversation, and what you should say while you pace outside on the phone with that shrewy voice.

As I get older, there's almost nothing I can hold back, and it's thrilling like crack cocaine to speak what I think while others tremble with the fear of their thoughts. On the tennis courts last year

I was asked to give up my lesson, ten minutes in, to a man who showed up late and who booked weeks after me. The bile burned my chest, a boiling kettle I could not contain, and I watched from above as I escalated unrest until a polite girl from Connecticut became a woman of planetary power, channeling generations of plutonian pissed-off-ness into a ringing, singing, joyful hymn of madness that echoed around the red clay courts and off the Hudson River, a crescendo of chauvinism squashed with a voice that belonged to — I don't know who, but she looked like me.

"I'm angry," she said. First, just out loud.

"I'M ANGRY," she yelled, operatic in the crowd. "I'm not leaving," she panted, red-faced, crazy, sweating, but sure.

And the men parted, with little ado, and the thing I said that I didn't *not* tell you was told as bold as lightning, mixed with estrogen. And I hit the ball.

 PROMPT: Write about a time you bellowed the truth.

The Hardest Thing

Nancy Kramer

The oppressive humidity of an Ohio summer offers the gift of juicy tomatoes and the sweetest corn you'll ever taste. "Knee-high by the Fourth of July," as the saying goes. We stop to see how high the corn is growing in early July in the fields just outside of town. It is a signal of the quality of the crop to be harvested in the next few weeks, prior to the annual state fair.

The summer heat and humidity make me, a fair-skinned, light-haired, blue-eyed child, feel sick to my stomach. My mother makes me wear an itchy straw hat to avoid sunburn and applies lots of Sea & Ski sunscreen. My blood type attracts mosquitoes; twenty-one bites on one leg this summer. The lightning bugs are my friends. I catch them in mason jars and stuff grass in the jar, poke holes in the top, and put the jar next to my bed so they will shine their magical lights in my room. The old gray window fan blowing on me helps me make my way to sleep.

As I grow older, I find ways to be out of the heat of the house as much as possible. We cannot afford air-conditioning. I spend most summers at the pool and the library, and, once I turn sixteen, working as a cashier at our local Kroger grocery store. My mother has said I have to go to college, but my family can't afford to send me. I end up working full-time at Kroger to pay for my tuition, room, and board while going to the only university I am ever exposed to, Ohio State, based in my hometown of Columbus.

It is 1975, the summer between my sophomore and junior years of college. I have returned from living independently on campus for the first time in my life and am now back in our family home for the summer. My father helped me buy a used Chevy Camaro (not my choice) with white leather interior (not my choice) that he then enthusiastically had painted an egregious teal color (not my choice). It is a horrible paint job by Earl Scheib — the guy who's advertising campaign is: "I'm Earl Scheib, and I'll paint any car, any color for $29.95." My dad is proud of what he has done for me, and I live to make my dad proud.

The Kroger store where I work is near the campus of Ohio State, very convenient during school but a thirty-minute drive for me to get home during the summer months. Our family home is a one-thousand-square-foot redbrick ranch house with a kitchen, a living room, three bedrooms, and one bathroom, plus an unfinished basement. There is no garage. On this evening after a 3 p.m. to 10 p.m. shift, I pull into our driveway at almost 11, parking behind our family's royal blue Ford Galaxie.

Something doesn't feel right. I enter through the side screen door into the kitchen. The lights are off and only a single candle is flickering atop the kitchen table, which is covered in a vinyl tablecloth. It's a hot, sticky night, and I hear the singing of the cicadas in the distance. The mood is ominous.

Standing at the doorway in my gold Kroger smock over my brown polyester uniform top and pants, I find my father sitting at the table nursing his whiskey. I've never seen him at the kitchen table by himself. My mother is always with him. They often say they are having "nightclub," which is code for, "We can't afford to go out, so we are going to sit here and drink the heavy stuff, chat, and smoke the night away with our unfiltered Camels."

I come in and ask, "What's going on? Why are you sitting there all alone?"

My father's voice is unusual as he answers me. "While you were working at Kroger today, your mother went into your room. She went through your stuff and found a letter you wrote to your boyfriend."

I gulp and feel my face getting hot.

"The letter wasn't sealed, so she read it. You talked about your relationship and that you had slept with him. She got really upset and took a bunch of Valium. I had to take her to the hospital to have her stomach pumped so she wouldn't die.

"It wasn't right that she looked at your stuff," he continued, "but what you did and wrote wasn't right either."

My face gets hot. I begin to sweat. Suddenly I feel like I can't breathe. Tears roll down my face.

I turn away and walk blindly to my bedroom, which is jammed with a bed, dresser, and desk that were my mother's furniture as a young child. I'd painted the once-white furniture dark blue and then "antiqued" it with a black overcoat. I fling myself on the small bed, and there, on top of my dresser's embroidered linen runner, lies the letter to my college boyfriend. I desperately want to leave the house, but there is nowhere to go. Plus, it is past my curfew.

As I lay on my bed staring at the ceiling, I am despondent. For as long as I can remember, my parents and the teachings of the

Catholic Church have set life expectations for me, dictating how I am to behave. In our world, I have sinned.

I glance at the crucifix hanging on my bedroom wall, Jesus's open wounds and crown of thorns. The young girl in me has a flashback of the image I visualized so often in Catholic school: me burning in hell standing next to the devil, surrounded by flames from the fire at my feet. I was not to have sex before getting married. How am I going to make this right?

Viscerally, at my core, I feel paralyzed by my stress. The events of that night are never spoken about again. Never.

The experience creates a trap that I live in for the next twenty-five years.

Two years later, despite my misgivings, I marry my college boyfriend in a picturesque Christmas wedding. We begin to build a life together, and ultimately have three incredibly wonderful, beautiful children.

But unconsciously, I will begin to create a parallel professional existence outside my personal life. Within four years of my wedding, I will start my own business, with a then-little-known company called Apple Computer as my first client. I break through cultural barriers as a female entrepreneur in the 1980s. My company will become the largest independent female-owned advertising firm in the country. Our creative work receives national and international recognition. We are recognized as a best place to work by the *Wall Street Journal*, *Working Mother* magazine, and others. I will even have a brief personal relationship with Steve Jobs.

In 2000, I will appear on CNN, CNBC, and other networks, talking about how the internet is changing consumer shopping habits — and how someday (yes, someday) we are going to buy products and services on the internet. I am recognized as an Entrepreneur of the Year, featured in *Fast Company*, *Business Week*, and *Inc.*, and designated one of the "100 Most Influential Women in Advertising History."

Along the way, I will achieve many industry firsts, from creating Apple's first interactive retail experience, to launching Victoria's Secret online — an event memorialized in a time capsule at MIT — to creating the first way to buy something in a social media stream, which received a US patent. I create and produce two iconic Super Bowl commercials. I even testify in front of Congress on the importance of workplace equality policies. I serve on dozens of boards — some public, some private.

Everything seems perfect. I am living a bigger, more adventurous life than I ever could have imagined, filled with incredible people and meaningful work.

But my inner life is filled with deep despair. In truth, I am stuck in 1975, the night of my mom's suicide attempt and the personal choices I felt forced to make in the days, months, and years that followed.

Over two decades, I live in fear of being outed. Outed for living a lie, outed for being the dumb blonde my mother told me I was all my childhood, outed for not loving my husband, outed for pouring all my emotional energy into by business. My mother, my husband, my colleagues, my clients, my family — when are they going to realize that I'm faking it all? More importantly, when am I going to be able to acknowledge the dual lives I have created, and the subsequent consequences?

Some nights my inner pain is so great I fantasize about driving my car off the road and into a wall. I am barely holding it all together.

Something's got to change. Something's got to give. Or else something's going to break.

And then it does.

Everything. My marriage. My business. My body. Myself.

 PROMPT: Something's got to give or something's going to break.

Music Lessons

Steve Kemper

"I *love* this song," said Jude, turning up the car radio.

The singer, a tough woman addressing her lover, declared that she had to be free, no strings attached, and if he couldn't live with that, he could "hit the road, Jack."

I looked over at her in the driver's seat and smiled. *OK*, I thought, *message received*. Jude and I had been seeing each other for a couple of weeks. Metaphorically speaking, she had one hand on my neck pulling me toward her and the other on my chest pushing me away. A mixed message, but I could work with ambiguity. I had plans for us, a whole pocketful of strings.

I saw the first sign of this in myself on a dance floor at a club...I'll come clean: at a disco, where I wouldn't have been caught dead if not for Jude. I was a jazz-club guy, a foot-on-the-rail blues guy, but she loved to dance, so I went to — this is still hard to admit — the disco, and danced with her to dumb ditties. While the music *tinka-boomed* and a high toneless voice sang, "Fly away like a 747," I knew, watching her move, sexy and self-conscious, that if it came to it, I'd even dance to the Bee Gees, as long as I could do it with her.

We met in October, and I made her a sumptuous French dinner with apples and cream while John Coltrane warmed my apartment. Afterward, when I moved to the couch, Jude chose the rocking chair, where she could keep some space between us and move to her own rhythms.

Message received, I thought, and then I put on Sarah Vaughan singing "I've Got the World on a String," taking luscious risks with the melody. "Lucky me, can't you see," she sang huskily, "I'm in love." Jude crossed her legs and rocked more briskly.

We went to the disco again and smoked cigarettes even though neither of us really smoked, particularly me, who choked and coughed, which made her laugh. And then I said, feeling a little more sure of her now, that it was actually a gag response to Donna Summer, which made her laugh harder.

On a crisp night in early November, we snuck into a college party hall, where the music sounded like metal tearing. We couldn't dance, couldn't listen, couldn't talk, so we escaped into the quad and kissed there, the prelude to something.

Not long after, I spent the night for the first time, and we fumbled around, playing the usual bedroom overtures to the main movement. But at what should have been the crescendo, I, to my dismay and bewilderment, understood precisely what an elder friend meant when she said that ever since her husband started the blood pressure pills, sex had been like trying to stuff a marshmallow into a piggy bank.

"So," I said, after pausing for a few awkward beats, "was it good for you too?" She threw back her head and laughed, bless her.

At the beginning of December, late one night, we drove for an hour to get buttered rum at an inn I knew, perched high overlooking a lake. But the inn was closed, so I grabbed her, and we danced without music on the wide, empty porch, among the leaves dancing in the wind.

Sometimes she cooked for me now, pastas in rich sauces, and we ate while listening to Bach and Mozart explore the possibilities for harmony in counterpoint. I made her brandied chicken and pears in red wine, and amused her by imitating João Gilberto's seductive Brazilian accent doing Gershwin: "S'wondare-fool, s'mar-vo-loze, that you should care for me. You make my life so gla-mo-rose, you can't blame me for feeling am-o-rose."

By the middle of December, when the air was sticky with Christmas carols, we both knew that we had come to a turning point, that it was time to break our strings or compose something with them. Then a few days before Christmas, I suddenly needed to have a disc removed from my back. I joked that she had wrenched my spine by pulling me one way and pushing me another. When she visited me at the hospital on Christmas Eve, she looked exasperated. When she had left work, she intended to turn right, toward home, but her arms turned the wheel left, toward me. "S'won-dare-fool," I crooned, "s'mar-vo-loze."

A few nights later, sitting naked together on my couch, celebrating my release from the hospital with champagne, pâté, and candles, she asked about my guitar, why I never played it. I told her I never played for anyone except myself. She asked me to play for her.

"Little darlin'," I sang for her, "it's been a long cold lonely winter. Little darlin'," I sang to her, "it seems like years since it's been clear." She was listening with her whole body. Music made from strings. "Little darlin'," I sang, "I think the ice is slowly melting. Here comes the sun. Here comes the sun. It's all right."

Her eyes were soft. We kissed. *Message received.*

 **PROMPT:** Music lessons

Freedom or the Grave

Gerald Yukevich

As a young emergency room physician in a small hospital a few miles north of Boston, I had just failed to resuscitate a wiry gentleman in his late eighties, an Irish immigrant and a beloved hospital employee. Call him Tim.

Tim was freshly dead, and I felt an odd impulse to kiss him. That evening when he had clutched his chest and collapsed in the parking lot, we ran out with a stretcher and retrieved him. Twice over the previous year, we had brought Tim back from death, but this time his old Irish heart and lungs had truly and finally given up.

The priest came in and anointed Tim's forehead. His daughters in Chicago and Detroit were notified. His body, cooling down to room temperature, lay waiting for the funeral director to come and cart him away.

I leaned over him and scouted out a spot on his wrinkled forehead to kiss, not far from where the priest's thumb had drawn the oil cross. But I hesitated; a nurse and the janitor were still in the room. They no doubt wondered why I stood there in a trance, mutely lingering over Tim's body, while other patients waited for me.

For historical context, it was 1981, the first year of Reagan's presidency. A few months before in Northern Ireland, the famous protester Bobby Sands of the Provisional Irish Republican Army had dominated international headlines. Sands and nine other fellow hunger strikers had died in Maze prison, near Belfast. The world had watched the vigil in dread, and the defiant Maze prison hunger strikers were now famous martyrs for the cause of independence.

The Irish troubles were on many people's minds then, especially in Boston, where sympathy for the rebels waxed strong. We heard rumors of locals running American guns to Ireland, and the bomb that blasted Lord Mountbatten's fishing boat two summers before was still in the public's consciousness. Boston's Irish loyalists seemed reluctant to condemn the assassination of that distinguished and despised Windsor.

What put me in a trance that evening, as the nurse and janitor eyed me curiously, was the irony of Tim's death.

To most hospital employees, Tim had been a lovable, often cranky curmudgeon. Short, lean, pink-faced, and with a slow, arthritic gait, he whistled and muttered to himself in his thick Irish brogue, as he puttered about the hospital as the resident handyman. He kept his cube-shaped head at an angle, and he often winced in pain when he moved his neck. His flattened nose, the apparent result of early facial trauma, angled westward.

For over four decades, Tim had fixed leaky pipes, mended floor-waxing machines, puzzled over electrical short circuits, maintained the boiler and the air-conditioning units, mowed the lawn, and served as the ingenious troubleshooter for all the little hospital's technical problems.

In the summer and fall, Tim also supplied an abundant variety of vegetables to the hospital cafeteria from his own garden, whose bell peppers and tomatoes, he boasted, were the finest anywhere outside of Ireland.

Since his American wife had passed away ten years before, Tim had taken most of his meals in the hospital cafeteria, where I enjoyed chatting with him. I never forgot to compliment him on his vegetables, a gesture he appreciated. Though he spoke reluctantly of his life before he came to America, he once confided a poignant personal story.

What the nurse and janitor looking curiously at me that evening did not know was that Tim too had once made headlines as an Irish hunger striker. During the bloody rebellion of the 1920s, he had battled the Black and Tans in the streets and landed in prison. The sign posted over his jail cell announced in large letters: "Freedom or the Grave," a dire phrase he repeated to me in his gravelly voice more than once.

The ordeal in Dublin lasted many weeks. Tim was down to skin and bones. Starved and feeble, he was only days from perishing as a patriotic martyr. But here I was, sixty years later, looking down at the remains of a feisty and remarkable fellow who had survived quite vigorously and cantankerously to a very ripe age.

How had it happened that Tim was spared martyrdom in Dublin?

"You see, while I was lying in the cell, a lovely young woman from Boston came in and interviewed me for her newspaper. She said she had seen my headlines and wanted to tell my story."

"That's how you met your wife?" I'd asked.

"She said if I stopped my strike, she'd take me back to Boston and marry me."

"Right on the spot?"

"Well, it took a few interviews. But she was persistent. The third time she came back, I realized I was falling in love."

"And she helped get you out of Ireland?"

"The authorities figured if they kicked me out of the country, I'd stop being a pain in the rear end for them."

"So they let you out?"

"You're talkin' to me, Doctor, aren't you? Or am I just an illusion?"

"Did you ever have any second thoughts?"

"Doc, if you had ever met my wife, you'd understand why I'm the luckiest man alive. I loved that woman more than I hated the Black and Tans. Call me selfish, but it's true."

Tim's front teeth were crooked, and so was his smile. But when he said those words, his blue eyes bored straight into me.

Love had conquered hate, a simple and beautiful story.

There was a knock on the door. The funeral director and his assistant had arrived to remove Tim. I watched as they read the death certificate and then transferred him over to their stretcher. As they pulled the sheet over Tim's face, I realized I had missed my chance. It was time for me to go and see the other patients.

Now, forty years later, I regret I did not give Tim a goodbye kiss on the forehead. But at other times in my practice since then, when all I had to offer a dying patient was a kiss, I have not hesitated. Thanks, Tim.

 PROMPT: Write about one regret you have.

Father's Day

Colin McEnroe

By 11 a.m. Sunday, I could tell this was going to be a day that stretched itself out.

I took some newspapers out on our shady deck, but I couldn't concentrate well enough to read a short book review.

I settled on the crossword puzzle. The unspoken assumption of a crossword puzzle is that you know at least some of the answers, which is not how I feel on Father's Day.

Declan the dog followed me onto the deck and flung himself down. He rarely lets me out of his sight. It occurred to me that he has been drafted into some roles dogs were never meant to play.

Facebook was to be approached gingerly if at all. Too many pictures of happy fathers. Too many tributes from grateful sons and daughters.

There is an underworld, a stratum below these holidays. The lovelorn may dread Valentine's Day. The pervasively lonely may feel especially rebuked during the November and December holidays.

This was the year I realized that Father's Day had become a labyrinth for me.

Three years ago, my son had become very ill. That is almost everything I can say about it. He is fierce about his privacy, and many other things have been stripped away from him. When his diagnosis was given, I prepared myself for his death. What came for him instead was an almost incomprehensible swarm of Furies — hornets of both the body and the mind.

He was never, from the age of ten, one to look at the bright side. As an adolescent and very young adult — ten or twelve years before his illness struck — he developed the unsettling habit of telling people he wouldn't live beyond forty. Milton has Satan say, "The mind is its own place, and in it self / Can make a Heav'n of Hell, a Hell of Heav'n." My son, it could be said, has a confirmation bias toward hell, and the last three years have given him a lot of raw material to work with.

He is alone a lot, unwilling to leave the house. His heroic mother visits him many nights. I'm the relief pitcher two nights a week. He is angry about his fate. Believing in no god and having meager contact with anyone else, he is often mad at us.

Are you getting a sense of how I feel about Father's Day? There are fathers who have it worse. On Sunday, I thought a lot about the fathers of Sandy Hook and Uvalde. The underworld has many chambers, some darker than others.

I also thought, sitting on the deck, about Thomas Nagel, the philosopher who wrote the famous essay "What Is It Like to Be a Bat?" One of Nagel's central points is that he can sort of imagine what it would be like (for him) to be a bat. But he can never understand what it is like for a bat to be a bat.

This is part of a much larger argument about consciousness, but let's skip that for now. We live subjectively. Each of us is a human trying to understand the experiences of other humans, who might as well be bats. Rilke says that love is "two solitudes [that] protect and touch and greet each other." That's as close as we get to being "as one."

I drove over to see my son that night, night being the only time he is willing to receive us. He was having new(ish) bodily sensations. They worried him. We talked for a long time about what to do. What to do about these symptoms. And, generally, what to do. What to do?

Unprompted by me, he said no one could understand what his life has been like. I agreed. I told him his mother and I do try, but we have no way of truly feeling his feelings.

That meant something to him. He said he was sorry that Father's Day had been derailed. I told him we would do it another night. He told me he appreciates what I do for him. Each of us said we loved the other.

Going home means driving over Avon Mountain in the dark. It was 12:11 when I reached its crest. The winding road seemed less precarious than usual. I was a little lighter in my soul.

Things had worked out reasonably well, within the strange frame that holds the painting of our current lives.

I'd let him be a bat. It felt like a gift to both of us.

 **PROMPT:** Father's Day

Eating Your Grief

Nancy Slonim Aronie

"What was your grief food?" my friend Cindy says, as I am handing her the black bean soup I have brought as my offering, in what I know must be her darkest hour. Condolence calls are awkward at best. Cindy tells me she has three more bean soups on the porch. I see they are lined up like planes on a runway waiting for takeoff. "But mine has coconut and lime," I whine. "And ginger," I add, "so I hope I get moved to the front of the pack." Actually, I don't care where my soup ends up. I just wanted to make her laugh.

After a brief visit, where I chattered about the lousy March weather and the ugly refrigerator we were just forced to buy, I found myself doing what the French call *l'esprit de l'escalier*, literally translated "the spirit of the staircase," meaning, thinking of the perfect reply too late. "What was your grief food?" my friend had asked me. Did I not answer because I didn't want to think of what food I ate when my son Dan died and have to face my own grief, or did I not want to face hers? Did she ask because she wanted to put me at ease because she knew we were now both members of the same club, a club no one wants to belong to? And why, oh why, did I want to make her laugh?

It's hard to drive while kicking yourself, but I managed to do both, at the same time thinking, *Why didn't I say, 'I can't even remember what I ate, what people brought. I can't remember what nourished me. I can't remember anything'?* It was twelve years ago. What I can remember is, one minute I was the mother of two sons, and the next minute I was the mother of…well, ya see, there's one of the interesting problems. When people say, "How many kids do you have?" should you say, "Past tense or present tense?" and really make them uncomfortable? Should you say, "I have two, but I lost one," as if he's wandering somewhere in aisle five at Cronigs? How easy it is to divert and avert pain with a snappy wisecrack.

I should have said, "The wedding cookies, the round balls with pecans and powdered sugar." But does that even qualify as my grief food? Maybe that's revisionist history. Maybe it was chopped liver on Ritz crackers. Who knows?

What I do know is that as a culture we are toddlers in terms of how we deal with other people's grief. And you would think since I went through it, I'd be better at it.

My standard note over the years has included "there are no words."

I recently read an article in *The Atlantic* that kind of made me wince.

The father writing the piece had lost two teenagers in a car wreck. He addressed most everything everyone has already written about: fear of saying the wrong thing in case it makes the bereaved break down and start crying uncontrollably, people not mentioning their own loss for fear of causing more pain, fear of the grief triggering their own unexpressed grief. He wrote, "Almost everyone we knew landed on the same unfortunate solution: 'There are no words.'"

Oops. I gulped and kept reading as he proceeded to say that "there are no words" acts as a conversation killer just when what you want is a conversation.

I think back, and all the love and hugs and cards and food were comforting, but what comforted me most and still do are stories about Dan. When I bump into someone who says, "I was a nurse at the ER. I loved Dan. We all did."

I have been approached on Circuit Ave., in line at the Steamship Authority, walking on Lucy Vincent Beach, by folks who saw Dan do his stand-up at Wintertide in the seventies or worked with him at one of his many summer jobs or had a brief but passionate love affair with him.

Those kinds of encounters are the healing I forgot when I visited my friend yesterday.

At least I didn't say what Cindy and I both agreed were the worst attempts, like, "He's in a better place," or, "Time heals all wounds." The "better place" would be alive and with me. And I don't know what time heals, besides maybe a paper cut.

The thing is, everyone grieves differently. You have to come up with your own thoughtful, comfortable response because, as my friend Laura Lentz says, "It's easier to walk with grief than to bury it."

I may still say, "There are no words." I may still bring bean soup. But one thing I know for sure: I will not pretend I am there to talk about ugly refrigerators and the weather.

 PROMPT: What's your grief food?

I Want to Be Water

Elizabeth Lesser

I have been wracking my brain on how to be part of something helpful during these times. It's a tinderbox out there! I want to be water. I want to "love thy neighbor" — even the one with the lawn sign that makes my blood boil; the one whose TV is always set to the "other" news station; the one who won't vote; the one who will, but for _____??!! I *want* to be water, but I fail at magnanimous feelings and inclusive behavior every day. The divisions have become so sharp, even between people who previously agreed on almost everything. Land mines everywhere. How do we walk out of this mess without blowing each other up? Certainly not via the takedown culture of social media. What's the point of smearing our opinions all over the electronic landscape if it only fortifies the ramparts separating us?

Sure, I am working for the candidates I want to see elected; I am writing about the issues I care about; I am donating to causes I believe in. But I am beginning to think that the most effective thing I can do as one human being in these hot times is to respond to everyday situations with small acts of cooling kindness. Like, speaking up when the woman in the long line at the grocery store yells at the checkout guy, blaming him for making her late while demanding that he bags her large purchase.

"It's not really his fault," I gingerly tell the outraged woman. She mumbles an excuse and leaves quickly. I'm next in line. I thank the clerk for serving us. He says there just aren't enough people who want to work at the store, so the lines are long. "We get it," I say. Several people waiting on the line nod their heads and offer their own thanks to the clerk. He looks stunned by the recognition that he's an actual person and not a robot ringing up the groceries. This changes the atmosphere in our little group of shoppers; there's a palpable sense of connection among strangers, as if we just woke up from a trance.

We're all in a trance these days. We forget our shared humanness. I certainly do. Just this morning I found my blood pressure rising while on hold with the doctor's office, listening to the annoying music and the absurdly untruthful recording that says — over and over — "Your call is important to us." *Oh yeah? Then why have I been waiting for twenty minutes just to renew a prescription?* When the overworked receptionist finally picks up, I want to scream. But I don't.

I take a deep breath and observe my reactivity. That's what I've been practicing on the meditation cushion for years — to pause before reacting; to question my instincts and assumptions; to *be* the peace and the kindness that I long to see in the world. But what's the point of meditation if I can't use it in real life? So, before taking my frustration out on the receptionist, I breathe. I pause. I put my hand on my heart, and I ask her how's she doing. She immediately softens her defensive stance. She's helpful. She apologizes for the wait and thanks me for my patience.

Later in the day I mail a package at our dilapidated local post office. The nasty postal worker everyone loves to complain about doesn't even look up as he chides me for not using an official postal service box, saying something under his breath about "entitled out-of-towners." I'm about to say something snide back, like, *I've lived here longer than you, buddy.* But instead, I say, "Hey, Jim, it's me! Remember? Our kids used to play soccer together."

He looks up. Our eyes meet. "Oh yeah, I remember you," he says. "I have grandchildren now!"

"Me too. Can you believe it?"

We both laugh. He's shaken out of the trance, out of his reactive storyline about city hipsters who look down on him and bitch about the broken US Postal Service as if he has any control over it. "Hey, next time use the right mailer," he says, sounding almost friendly.

I can't always pull off this good behavior. Some days are better than others. But my intention, my practice, my prayer is to be water, especially to my own hot reactivity. This doesn't mean there aren't some very bad players in our personal and collective lives who need to be brought to justice, or stripped of power, or walked away from. It doesn't mean I will dampen my passions or abandon my core values. It means only that I don't want to let my values and passions create a cascade of more problems, more conflict, more division.

I'm not expecting perfection — of myself or others — just the intention to be a light spring rain every now and then. Just the prayer that one act of love might ripple outward and join other rivulets that run together into an ocean of empathy and sanity. As this year's fiery election cycle in the US heats up, we are going to need as much cooling down as possible. Let's help each other be water.

 PROMPT: Write about a time you were either water or fire.

Explore a Universal Theme

Universal themes make a piece universal (surprise, surprise). If your essay is about raising piglets in Zambia, I'm going to have a hard time becoming interested unless you bring the essay around to something I can relate to. Maybe how you were a kid on a farm and your grandfather let you keep a baby pig, or you refused to eat pork when you were four and you still don't eat pork, but you remember something your kindergarten teacher said when she was reading *The Three Little Pigs*. I don't care what the reference is, but lead me to something emotionally familiar, even if only for a quick minute. Then you can go back to your esoteric story.

Give me a weaving of relatable images, themes, and memories that overlap and intertwine.

So if you want me in, I am a sucker for romance, for a hard-luck story, an underdog, food, sex, drugs, raising kids, marinating chicken thighs, getting cataract surgery, being in a car wreck, finding a divorce lawyer — something that pulls me in. But if you are just informing me, giving me facts and information, with lots of exposition but nothing personal, then it's an essay but not the kind we're talking about here. This book is about the *personal* essay with the universality that forces my heart to open, that makes me feel like I know you, I *am* you, and all I want for you is ease and safety and happily-ever-after. That doesn't necessarily mean a tidy ending. It just means including a theme that makes me fully yours.

The universal theme is about our human connectedness to one another and to our world.

The City I Ride In

Naomi Beinart

I take the express train twice a day, forty minutes each way, and not to brag, but I know all the tips and tricks. The New York City that you see on promotional ads with friendly taxis and reasonably priced soft pretzels, that's not the city I ride in. The city I ride in is a documentary of betrayal, a chalkboard of evidence showing how the government and the people in charge have failed. Scraps of unwashed clothes slouch off the unwashed bodies that sleep on pastel benches on the train. People without homes, 7-Eleven Big Gulps extended, plead for dimes and nickels. Humans tell humans: "Homeless and hungry. Please help." The passersby walk briskly, trying to avoid their guilt and the smell. "I'm busy, I don't have money on me, sorry," usually expressed with eyes glued to a cellphone.

I am not a particularly good person. I do not open my wallet every time. I do not always make eye contact. Maybe it seems like I don't care enough, and maybe that's true. But there is also an undeniable anxiety that sits next to me twice a day. I glance nervously when waiting for the train because every week, it seems, there's a report that someone has been pushed onto the tracks. This morning, below the headlines on world affairs, I read about stabbings on the 4 Train. I'm thankful I don't take that route, until I remember that months before, a shooting happened on my train, the express. I wonder if the person screaming obscenities nearby might be armed.

I know this isn't fair. I know that almost all the people who live without homes are not dangerous or guilty of anything other than being poor. I believe that if a small fraction of my homeless co-riders act erratically, it's likely because they've been abandoned by a country that has denied them the care they need. Every time I give money to those who need it, I know I've done the right thing.

Still, my anxiety sometimes consumes me, drowns me until I need to pause my music and chip my nails to regain my composure.

There's a fine line between fear and guilt. My fear comes from being a teenage girl with spandex shorts and a ponytail, on my way to volleyball practice. I'm hoping to make varsity and not encounter danger along the way. My guilt comes from being a white person who has the money to buy someone a bottle of water. My kneepads cost twenty-five dollars, and the person sleeping six seats away probably hasn't eaten breakfast since Thursday. I don't know what part of myself I should listen to: the part that will make me a better person or the part that will keep me safe. When I keep my distance, am I protecting myself or protecting my privilege?

My Take

This is such a universal theme: guilt vs. fear.

Considering Naomi is a fifteen-year-old author, I hope you're as blown away by her writing as I am.

From that first sentence, I'm engaged. I love "not to brag," as if she were talking with her friends. It's conversational in the best possible way.

The combination of "friendly taxis and reasonably priced soft pretzels" is great writing. As I've mentioned earlier, I love when a writer combines two very different images in one sentence. To illustrate combining very different words and how well that works, I often tell my students the story of my neighbor and my wine.

We live in a dry town, so I always have a few bottles of wine in case someone comes over or we are invited to dinner somewhere. I don't drink wine, but my neighbor does. I do eat Marshmallow Fluff. And she always has a jar sitting on her pantry shelf. If I come home and find a bottle of wine missing, I know Elizabeth has come over and snagged/borrowed/grabbed one of the aforementioned. By the same token, I have been known to saunter over across the stone wall and return home with my guilty pleasure.

I don't have a lock on my door. So one particular night I was reading on the couch, eating the Fluff, when someone burst through the door. My first thought was, *OMG, I probably have white guck in the corners of my mouth, and here I am, holding on to a jar of fructose. This is so embarrassing.* But my next thought was, *Oh, but I'm reading Tolstoy. I know 100 percent that Tolstoy and Marshmallow Fluff have never been in a sentence together.* There. Listen. Those three words just sang you an aria. Just like Naomi's pretzels and taxis.

Then she writes, "The city I ride in is a documentary of betrayal, a chalkboard of evidence showing how the government and the people in charge have failed." These word choices are unique and powerful.

"Scraps," "slouch," and "sleep" — nice alliteration.

Using "pastel" to describe the subway benches is original. And original is what we are always looking for. She could have used "faded yellow" or "light brown" or any number of predictable words to describe the seats, but "pastel" has a gentler feel, and I think she is getting to the vulnerability of the passengers.

"7-Eleven Big Gulps extended" is visual. Most of us know what those huge plastic cups look like.

"Plead" is a powerful word. It's desperation. I feel it.

"Guilt" and "smell" are words that pull at each other.

When she quotes the messages the passersby say, like, "I'm busy…sorry," and then adds, "with eyes glued to a cellphone," the reader feels several responses at once. Anger: How could these people not care? Guilt: How many of us haven't looked the other way when asked for money at some point? And compassion: We don't want to think of ourselves as someone who would look down at their phone, yet we empathize with those people, as well as with the person in need.

"I am not a particularly good person" conveys the vulnerability that I think is the most important part of a personal essay. Then the line "anxiety that sits next to me" is perfect.

The repetition of "I know" in the next paragraph is powerful because it's intentional.

They're "not dangerous or guilty of anything other than being poor" is wise and generous and smart and sensitive and kind. We want to love the narrator. And here we do.

The line "Every time I give money" tells us she gives regularly. She's not bragging. She's explaining, and it makes us feel close to the narrator. She is a good person in addition to being humble about being good.

"Pause my music and chip my nails" are great details. She's a teenager. She doesn't have to say, "Hey, I'm only fifteen." She just showed it.

How about the wisdom of the line "There's a fine line between fear and guilt"?

"Spandex shorts and a ponytail" are terrific visual details. Then "I'm hoping to make varsity and not encounter danger along the way" followed by "my kneepads cost twenty-five dollars, and the person sleeping six seats away probably hasn't eaten breakfast since Thursday" is absolutely brilliant.

Finally, she wraps it up with her moral dilemma so that the reader asks the same question of herself: "When I keep my distance, am I protecting myself or protecting my privilege?"

What a thrill to read a young person's take on their inner journey. I can't wait to see what this kid is gonna do next!

 PROMPT: Write about the fine line between fear and guilt.

Ten Days Just Being a Writer

Kathy Gunst

Ten days is a long time when you're not thinking about anything else. Like laundry. Like putting away the dishes. Like what you'll make your husband for dinner. Like what you need to pick up from the grocery store. Like when copy is due for your next radio show. Like who you haven't called or emailed back yet. Like how many likes you have on your last Instagram post. Like who posted on Facebook. Like do you even care about social media? Like how your daughter is doing in her eighth month of pregnancy with your first grandchild. Like how your other daughter is doing in steamy LA with her work and relationship. Like did you pay that last credit card bill? Like is there enough in your checking account to cover it? Like did you actually make it to the post office and mail that box back or just think you did? Like did you weed the garden and water the houseplants? Like will anyone water them when you're gone? Like how long you have to finish the article you promised you would finish before you got here to become a writer for ten days. Like will you produce enough work during these ten days to actually call yourself a writer? Like will you think of yourself as a writer and not the person who thinks all the other thoughts instead of putting her thoughts and sentences and words and feelings and memories and history onto this screen?

You let go of it all. You clear the giant table in your mind of all the debris that sits on it — cluttered, endless piles of stuff — and take a big old rag and swipe the surface clean, let it tumble to the ground without giving one actual f**k. And you greet that big empty desk, with its view of majestic, overgrown pines and glimpses of the lake, where Maine loons sing a song each evening and sometimes early morning as you sit here and don't think about all the stuff but focus on why you are here. Let yourself just sit and wonder what it is you want to say. And how you finally have this space, in your mind, on this desk, on this screen, on this day to actually say it. And then you start to say it.

And the first two days it flows out of you so easily it makes you weep. And the third day you wake up and there's a ten-foot wall in front of you, a big old stubborn I-won't-move-for-anything wall, and you fear it's over. You had your two days, and it was glorious, but now it's over. And you wonder what you will do with the next week and wonder if you should pack up and go home. And you stare down this wall. And you stare some more. And you leave the desk and walk down the dirt path on the hill for a long swim, and you don't worry if it's dangerous to be out there in the ripple waves of the lake after a night of wind, all alone without anyone knowing where you are because you feel the need to slap those ripples with your strong summer arms and move through that water. And when you get back to your desk, you find there's now only half a wall up. And you decide to write over it. And under it, until eventually that wall feels that it is living in such an inhospitable environment that it decides to just crumble. And here you are…again… at this desk with its view and the loons in the distance, and you are writing.

You give in to the way days feel intolerably long and also intolerably short. The way hours go by before you realize you have been lost in it all, the words, the structure, the way a story starts to emerge. The way you didn't think about agents and editors and readers and decided, instead, to write the story you want to read and the one you want to tell. The freedom of that very big thought. The way you hardly think about eating all day. The way hunger feels like an obligation and not a necessity. The way sentences and ideas replace menus in your head. The way a scrambled egg and toast feels like just the right dinner. And then, the exhilaration of getting into bed at night, a creaky old thing, and finding your thoughts all in one place, as if there's only one pocket in a dress, only one place to put your thoughts instead of a robe with a million endless pockets where all the thoughts get scattered. The holding all in one place. The way you drift off to sleep, thinking you never will, wondering if the story about your grandmother placed against the one about your mother is balanced? Or does it need some sort of segue? Not thinking about the list of things that need to be done the next day. But floating off into the night of deep, dark, endless sleep.

 ► **PROMPT:** What's your list of things that keep you awake at night?

A String of Fate

Phebe Grandison

My blood runs red like the blush in my grandfather's cheeks when he asks my grandmother to dance. My heart beats a rhythm to the *tap, tap, tap* against the windowpane of my grandmother's dorm room, where she looks up to find my grandfather throwing rocks at her window. The hidden golden strands beneath the brown in my hair mirror the golden band slipped over my grandmother's finger, and the freckles over my skin map the miles it took for my grandmother to follow my grandfather into the war.

My ears only know the sound of crashing waves and the blare of the horn of the ferry that takes me to an island in a hidden corner of the world. My nose only knows how to breathe in the salty sea air and the pine scent of the forests. My eyes tell me I'm home when I spot my grandparents' little house underneath a sky full of stars.

My hands are the same type of cold as my mother's when she holds her hand in my father's, and whenever she asks why his hands are always warm his reply is "I'm warmhearted."

My blood is now pumping and my heart is beating a rhythm that is too fast for the music playing in the gym. I was getting nauseated by the heat of the stuffy room and tried to think of a time when I knew nothing but the cold. A couple days ago, my friend and I ventured to the frozen lake outside my dorm room, the cold air biting our noses and cheeks. I saw the snow-dusted trees surrounding the lake, which made me think of my grandparents' pine-scented island, but once I slipped on my ice skates, the thought had slipped my mind.

I followed my friend out into the middle of the lake, praying I wouldn't slip and fall. As I tried to see what lay beneath the frozen water, I noticed tracks in the ice. Someone else must have skated here before, and here I was thinking this was my friend's and my secret adventure.

The sound of clapping from the gym took me out of my reverie I dodged past the sweaty bodies of dancers and made my way to you.

I'd seen you here a couple of times before. Something told me that the loud music and rush of bodies was not the reason my heart was doing little jumping jacks. You looked up when I approached, and I tried not to think about the blush forming on my cheeks when I asked you to dance.

You said yes and led me to the dance floor. My hand was cold but yours was warm, and I couldn't help but think my hand fit perfectly into yours. You asked about my week, and I told you of my skating adventure, which produced a laugh. "Those tracks in the ice were yours?" "Yes." Conversation turned to plans for the summer, and when I told you about my grandparents' island, you just had this knowing look. "You've been there before."

The dance ended, but before you left, you added, "Maybe I'll see you again." I spent the days wondering where your dorm window was and if there were any rocks around. My thoughts wandered to how we almost kept missing each other until I somehow managed to find you. Maybe me finding you was more than just chance. Maybe it was something like *fate*.

That night I should have just asked you what you thought about that encounter. Because I bet you would have just blamed it on circumstance.

I was walking with my friends when I saw you across campus.

Your arms were wrapped around a girl, and you two were staring into each other's eyes. The girl's hair was shimmering golden, and her porcelain skin was spotless. It was like what was keeping you together was more than your arms being wrapped around her. It was something like a string of *fate*.

I felt the insides of my chest being crushed, my daydreams slipping through my fingers like running water. I tried to compose my features and listen to whatever conversation my friends were having, while secretly wondering if any of them would catch on that a part of me was drifting away.

The walk back to my dorm was deafening. I entered the building and looked at myself in the mirror, obsessing over the tiny freckles that wrecked my skin and wondering why my hair was a boring brown and not a shimmering golden. I thought of my grandparents and my parents and tried to place myself in a love story unfolding like theirs, but I never got an answer I wanted. *Maybe I wasn't destined for anyone else. Maybe I was destined to be alone.*

I'm in the little house underneath the stars. Puzzle pieces are strewn across the floor, and books are grouped into piles. I keep expecting I'll find you here on the island, at the docks watching the crashing waves or at the town center shopping for groceries, even though I know it is unlikely. There's an empty space in my chest reserved for someone who will hold me, which sometimes fills me with aching. But then my dad makes a joke that my grandfather has cooked way too much food, and my brother is giving my mother a hard time for losing her glasses, and laughter fills the room, and I know I'll find ways to fill that empty space again. And again. And again.

 PROMPT: What are you homesick about?

My Unsung Hero

Linda Pearce Prestley

Who would have thought that she would be the one?

Not even three years old and a skinny little thing. Not cute and fuzzy. Not endearing.

Just nineteen pounds, all bones and sharp angles, bald patches on her head, palsy on the side of her tiny face. So silent as she rocks in a tiny plastic chair.

She is what brought us to this orphanage in Ukraine, thousands of miles from home. "Babies are in short supply," they say. But that's not what we came for anyway. *Been there, done that,* I thought, what with our older brood still at home and a baby daughter, home just a year from this very same place. Now this is her turn, one of their beautiful but not-so-wanted children that they are offering for a chance at life. They call it "winning the lottery," and she has the winning ticket.

I approach her slowly. Out of the corner of her eye, she sees me but doesn't make eye contact. She runs away as if for her very life. Peter laughs. Here he is at the age of fifty-six, giving in to my younger need to add to the family. To make a difference. To save a life. "She's the one," he says. But I'm not so sure. It takes all the cajoling and lollipops I can gather to get near her. In those moments, I know that this little person will not be easy. She will not fold into my seasoned arms or welcome my good intentions, as our baby did the year before. She will be different, and she makes that clear, through scowls and shrieks, whenever I come close. She has thrown down the gauntlet. I accept her challenge. Now we understand one another. Ignoring her protests, I lift her struggling little body to take her from this place. Forever.

Her name is Olga, and it comes as no surprise to find that she has special needs. Needs that in my spirit of generosity and save-a-life enthusiasm, I may have underestimated. Almost a feral creature, one who resists any attempts to connect. Each day, my overtures are rebuffed with the same tiny snarl that she expressed back in Ukraine. My mommy bag of tricks just doesn't work with her. For weeks, then months, she wails in the night and stuffs the corner of her blanket down her throat to suck. She snatches anything others have and runs with it. She hoards food in strange hiding places. She eats voraciously. I later learn that this is what happens when a child has been abandoned to hunger and cold, with her only instinct one of survival. She takes what she wants and gives nothing in return. *Well, at least she's consistent*, I tell myself, when I'm not tearing my hair out.

Time passes, though, and she starts to put meat on her bones. Her face fills out, her hair grows in, and her gait grows steadier. Her tantrums become less frequent. She begins to see me as more than a means to an end. I become a source for good things. She climbs on my lap and says nothing while we just rock. And rock. Like she's a tiny baby. I sense the beginning of something new.

She makes progress by leaps and bounds, yet it's clear that no amount of special education, therapy, and love will reverse the effects of her first two and a half years of deprivation. She is diagnosed on the autism spectrum, but that doesn't change who she is or how we see her. She is just another addition to the family, and just like those that came before, whatever she needs, she will get. Quirky and very funny, she thrives from all that she is immersed in, well on her way to being the best that she can be. But as always, I remind myself not to expect too much. Olga will always be a little different.

Finally, she is all grown up. Who would think that with all her quirks and idiosyncrasies, she would become such a gift? The caring one, the no-nonsense one, the one who builds me up, the one I can really count on.

"Mom, it's time to take a shower," she tells me. "I don't feel like it," I reply. "I'm too tired. My leg hurts too much." "Come on,

Mom, you have to," she says. At her insistence, I reluctantly climb from the bed. She finds my crutches and walks slowly with me into the bathroom. She wraps my leg in plastic, careful not to touch the wound from my surgery. Then she helps me step into the shower where she has steadied a chair for me to sit in. "It hurts too much," I cry. "You can do it, Mom," she encourages me.

But it's not just the pain she sees. I am embarrassed. I don't want to need anyone like this or for anyone to see me like this, and she sees that in my face. As she gently pours the shampoo into her palm and begins to wash my hair, she laughs, "Honest, Mom, I do this all the time in my job at the group home. It's just body parts." She doesn't seem to care that I'm more than a few pounds over-weight, she doesn't care that my body is not perfect, she doesn't care that I am short-tempered for no reason or that I sound whiny or ungrateful. She understands that I can't do anything for her right now, that our roles have reversed. Her job is to make it better for me, and she sees what needs to be done.

No longer the tiny waif rocking back and forth in that hopeless room. She's so much more. My unsung hero.

 PROMPT: Write about a time you experienced a role reversal.

Opposites Attract

Nancy Slonim Aronie

We've all heard the expression "opposites attract," and I have to admit that my husband and I are almost the perfect example of that phrase. And it was very obvious in what happened the other night.

Every so often, I jokingly quote a stanza from a poem by Sir John Suckling (honest to God, that's his name — I don't know how the poor guy made it through junior high). It was a poem I had to learn by heart in English Lit. I utter the lines if my man is looking tired or not responding to something I said in the animated way I need him to. It goes like this:

> Why so pale and wan fond lover?
> Prithee why so pale?
> Will, when looking well can't move her,
> Looking ill prevail?

In response the other night, my husband said, "What does that mean exactly?"

I said, "The guy's friend is giving him advice on courting some woman. He's saying, 'You couldn't get her when you were healthy. Why do you think you can get her looking sickly?'"

"No," my husband said, "it's the guy talking to the girl, accusing her of being out partying all night, which is why she looks so pale."

This is the part when I look at him and think, *Who are you?*

But then there are the times when he looks up at the sky and, in a voice filled with awe, says, "Just think: Our planet is revolving at nine hundred miles per hour and our galaxy is only one of billions of galaxies out there. Doesn't that blow you away?"

And I say, "I just want to see a shooting star."

And he says, "They're not stars, they're particles."

I say, "I'm cold," and he says, "How can you be cold? It's hot in here."

Lately he's been repeatedly asking me how I feel about being on the edge of extinction. And my answer varies. Sometimes I say I don't think I'm on the edge of extinction. Sometimes I say, "I'm not going to spend my time thinking about the end. I'm trying to live in the now."

And then he says, "There will be no *now* if we don't do something about this climate emergency."

I say, "Let's have the Tragers over for dinner next Saturday night," and he says, "We just saw people."

If we are invited somewhere and I can get him to agree to go, he says, "What time?" I say, "Six." He says in shock, "Six? Who eats at six?" If I say seven, he says, "Seven? Who eats at seven?"

If we go out to dinner, on the way home he says, "How much would that chicken have cost at Stop & Shop?" I say, "That's not the point. The point is we were in a beautiful place. We got *served*. We ate brussels sprouts with pomegranates. We would never make brussels sprouts with pomegranates." He says, "I could have bought five chickens for that price, and thank God we never make brussels sprouts with pomegranates."

These are not arguments. They're just different ways of being in the world.

It turns out, most of our differences don't pull at the fabric of our relationship. We are not opposites. In fact we're complements of each other. Ballast for each of our overindulgences.

He's right. Five chickens do equal the price of the check. And when I show him that pleasure has a comparable monetary value, he understands what I'm talking about. And I get that eating out is a huge luxury.

And once I explained the meaning of the poem, he said, "Oh, I get it."

I explain that when a person says, "I'm cold," no one can challenge how that person *feels*. Just because they feel differently. Feeling cold is not an opinion about temperature.

As for his awe of the universe and my casual indifference, and my being sort of an extrovert and his being sort of an introvert, we're just different.

The problem would be if we both dug in our heels as if we were right, which would clearly make the other one wrong.

A long time ago a very wise friend (and I'm sure you've heard this before) said, "Do you want to be right, or do you want to be happy?"

We agree on this one big thing: We have both chosen to be happy.

 PROMPT: How are you different from someone you love?

You Can Go Home Again

Laura Lentz

When my father died and we put my mother in Sunrise Facility in Atlantic City, it was as if my compass in my pocket couldn't find its north, and I lost my sense of belonging. Even though my boyfriend was in my car, and my eleven-year-old daughter was in my car, and we were headed to the airport, I said, "I need to see the home again where I grew up." I made a sharp left turn toward the maple trees and the birches, toward the crab apple tree where my first cat was buried.

My compass was leading me to W. Delaware Trail, the small one-story brick home with the bay window that once had magnificent gardens planted with grief and longing by my mother's hands. My mother who loved the spiders and the birch trees and the sky.

My mother who loved books and libraries and her husband.

And my daughter rolled her eyes. "Mom…what are you thinking? Nobody will let a stranger into their home."

I traveled down country roads and passed the Methodist church and the Episcopalian church and the Catholic church that wouldn't marry me because of my mother's abortion, and the bowling alley with the faded sign, where I played my first perfect game.

Very little had changed.

We passed the Medford Library and all the stories that saved my life.

We turned down Christopher Mill Road, where the giant owls often flew in front of my car at night on my way home — as if to say, *You can fly too.*

When I pulled up to that too-small home for six people, in my blue rental car, there was a man in his early to mid fifties, with a tool belt on, staring at my car.

I got out of the car, walked toward him, and said, "I'm Laura Lentz, and I grew up in this house, and my father just died. I'd like to see the inside of the home if you are comfortable with that."

And he said, "Oh my God! You're Gloria's daughter? She's famous. Wasn't she on Merv Griffin and Larry King?" I nodded. "Yeah, that's her." "Let me get my wife. She's in the pool."

And just like that, I wasn't a stranger.

A few minutes later, Beatrice emerged from the front door smelling like chlorine and summer and motherhood, with a towel wrapped around her beautiful plump body, and she said, "Oh my God, hun, you just lost your father?"

And this woman I never met pulled me to her wetness, and hugged me so tight, our breasts smashed — cause that's how women from my hometown hug — and she said, "Please come in. The house is a mess, but come on in."

And just like that, I disappeared into the past, and into belonging, and I was home.

We all went to the basement, and Joe showed me all my ex-boyfriends' names carved into the unfinished wood frames, each name crossed out, and he showed me my father's measurements and said he was a builder too and he'd left my father's penciled measurements to honor him.

And I saw the kitchen where every argument began, where the endless bills were sorted, that brown Formica kitchen table where my mother also typed her manuscript.

When we got to Beatrice and Joe's bedroom, which was once my parents' bedroom, I stood in the doorway and began to cry.

Thinking of all the nights I crawled into their bed, or all the mornings we had trouble waking my mother up because she was on a journalism deadline the night before.

Beatrice put her arm around me. She said, "Hun, I just lost my father too. Cry it out." And I put my head on her shoulder and asked her when her father died, and she said, "Ten years ago," and we both laughed and cried and laughed, because nobody can measure grief in time.

My mother's extraordinary gardens were gone, the crab apple tree was gone, the patio had been rebuilt, and as I walked out the front door and hugged both of them again, I realized this place and the people from this small town live inside me; I never left them behind.

I asked them if they were happy in the home, and they said in their thick Jersey accents, "Yeah, yeah, hun, we're all so happy."

Small towns and the people who stay in them never forget those who left. This first belonging we experience — whether it's family, friends, or another country — it's the glue that keeps our memories together. It's our first wisdom training — always welcoming us with open hearts and open arms, and sometimes wearing a tool belt and a too-small spandex bathing suit, just in case something inside us is broken and needs repair.

 PROMPT: Small towns

Song of My Father

Lara O'Brien

I planned to grieve my father's death. I imagined it to be in the forest of Vinalhaven, an island in Maine where my husband and son have purchased thirty acres to build summer cabins for the family, a place I had yet to meet. I thought it out. I'd go lie on the mossy forest floor and watch for an eagle. I'd heard they live in the evergreens of the Basin, an inlet off Vinalhaven.

When my father was younger, he loved John Denver, and I grew up on his music. On my first date with my husband-to-be, he showed me his record collection. It was enormous and alphabetized, ranging from Dylan to Hothouse Flowers, In Tua Nua to Christy Moore and Planxty, Van the Man to the Rolling Stones. "Impressive," I said. "Name your favorite song — I bet I have it," he said in that sure way of his. "John Denver, 'The Eagle and the Hawk.'" I doubted he'd even know it.

This sweet man jumped up, and a moment later the soaring notes of the song and the eagle's flight filled the room. *Well,* I thought, *here's a man who gets it — nature, hope for humankind, goals of being a better person, flying high.* Did I decide to marry him then? I may have.

This was a song my father had taught me to love, as I'd watched him play it and get lost in its beauty. And now it will forever be the song I remember him by. So, two weeks after my father's death, I planned to go to the forest floor, look to the sky, watch out for the eagle, and see him soar. I'm a sucker for signs. I asked my father for them before he died. Mad, right?

I found a silver feather on the road in Edgartown the day before a recent writing retreat, and I knew the retreat would be good for everyone on it, even though I was working through a tiredness I had never felt before, a complete draining of energy. But writing circles tend to give and give and give, so much goodness they hold me up. Just by writing together, we can feed each other good energy. Story building, narrative shaping, listening, we crack our hardness to soften.

I researched the five stages of grief. They are denial, anger, bargaining, depression, and finally acceptance.

I understand there's no good in anger. I could have been angry at the hospital for not admitting Dad faster. It was clear he was struggling, but they sent him home. When he went back some days later, it was in an ambulance. He didn't want the "fuss," but we knew he was in trouble. He fought a brave battle to come home.

A few days after, I felt a wave of guilt for not insisting he go in earlier, for not calling the ambulance and having him taken into the Covid care unit. But he was a no-fuss man, so we didn't make a fuss.

Now I can accept his death because we saw him take his final breath. He is gone but his spirit is with us, which is why I'm watching for the signs and the eagle.

I've learned that it's not about how we handle this raw grief, but how it handles us. Grief has a mind of its own. It jumps out of memories hidden deep in our minds — a cup of soup he served me, his beautiful hand, his belly laugh. A song, a thought, and he is here with me instantly. But with the memory comes a sudden violent WHACK, a physical belt to the senses, and the tears pour down.

For my planned grieving event in the forest, I cleared all other responsibilities to just be with my father and our memories. But something happened along the way. My husband was driving us to Maine to show me this new island where they say "lobs thah" as two words and those lobsters fuel the whole island's industry. He described in detail his recent inventory of trees to harvest and diggers to build with and land to conserve and even a place for me to write. He was so animated about the trails we would explore and the hikes we would take.

Then a WhatsApp pinged from my brother. It was a picture of my sister and me as very young children, with my father in the center, about twenty-six years old. I had never seen it before. And then it happened, that massive thud of pain — for the young man, for the little girls, for his love, for his life, and most of all, for our loss. BANG. Breathe. Breathe. Breathe. And the tears kept on coming. I am a constant well of them now.

So this is grieving, on its own terms. Banging the f**king breath out of my body and letting me draw in one breath at a time to continue to live. Oh, I see it now: This is what people call the grieving *process*.

A grief counselor friend wrote to me today: "Grief is like being out to sea in a small skiff. Sometimes there's gentleness and sometimes the winds howl, knocking one all over the boat."

Still, I can't wait to get to the forest floor to write and watch for the eagle. I can see him in my mind's eye, flying through shafts of light and past moving clouds.

 ► **PROMPT:** Write about softening a hardness.

What Would You Like to See Happen?

Kate Taylor

I was in Los Angeles in 1970, working with the British singer and music producer Peter Asher on my first album, *Sister Kate*. Though I loved beyond measure being in LA at this time, working and forming friendships with musicians who were on the cusp of becoming our most beloved musical icons, I was also homesick for my home base, Martha's Vineyard, Massachusetts.

I loved the natural world there, the ocean and the sunlight, the birds and the fish and my family and friends.

Taking a break from recording on what turned out to be one very special evening, Peter and I joined friends and a packed house at the Troubadour Tavern to witness the first American live and in-person appearance by the amazing Elton John.

He blew the roof off the place! During his set of songs from his just-released album *Tumbleweed Connection*, he sang a song that resonated especially deeply with me. It reminded me of my life on my island home.

That night I mentioned to Peter that I loved the tune and wished I could record it for my album. Peter told me that he knew

Elton's manager, that we could invite them over to his house, where I was staying, and that I might ask Elton if I could record the song for *Sister Kate*. Peter did, I did, and Elton said, "Yes, by all means!" (!!!)

We gathered in the studio with, among others, Carole King on piano, Leland Sklar on bass, John Hartford on banjo, and Linda Ronstadt on backing vocals. When done, we had our version of Elton John's song "Country Comfort" ready for inclusion on my album.

Some months later *Sister Kate* was complete, and a single was released to radio. I was back in LA putting a band together for my tour. My dad came out for a visit. We were driving along a freeway when he asked, "Kate, what would you like to see happen with this career you're embarking upon?" I replied, maybe tongue in cheek, "Dad, having grown up with four brothers, what I'd like is that when I start singing in the car and someone leans over and turns on the radio, that it be *me* on the radio."

He nodded, leaned over and turned on the radio, and it was *me* on the radio! I was singing our first single release, Elton John's "Country Comfort"!

What a life!

 PROMPT: Write a fantasy of yours as if it's happening in real time.

Conclusion

*W*hen I love a book I postpone reading the ending because I don't want it to end. And I'm so afraid the author will mess it up.

But then if the ending is gorgeous, I feel personally graced, fed with a feeling of completion as if I have finished a phenomenal meal, total nourishment, the best spa visit, the best belly laugh. The best life has to offer.

Something that ends well is a perfect "all's well."

So this is it, my loves. This is how it ends. Or maybe this is how it begins.

My hope is that after reading all these gorgeous essays, you have come to the same conclusion I have. That absolutely everybody, all humans — doctors, lawyers, First Nation chiefs, the little people, the big people, the unwashed masses, the ones who take three showers a day, the kings and the queens, the biggest influencers with the most followers, the TikTokers, the Tinder swipers, the windshield wipers, the Luddites, the uptights, *all of us* — have something in common: We are all living with some variation of a broken heart.

All of us, even though our stories are different and our details are different, and our levels of processing being human are different, we are all very much the same. We really are one. Everything is connected, so when you do something — anything good, bad, or ugly — it affects everyone. That statement is not to make you paranoid; it's to wake you up, make you aware that you are not in a vacuum, that we are one big organism. But we all have our individual one-of-a-kind stories.

And once you know someone's story, it becomes harder to see them as separate from you.

When I first got married, I tried really hard to love my mother-in-law, Asna, but she seemed cold and unavailable. I remember thinking, *She doesn't realize how great I am* (oh, the arrogance of it all) and *How am I going to get a meaningful connection with this woman, my husband's mother, whom he adores?*

One day, probably three years into the marriage, I asked her if I could interview her. I had no idea what I was doing, but luckily, I pay attention to my unexplainable impulses. She said yes, hesitantly.

She wore her hair in a very tight bun. I asked if I could take her hair down. Here, she was really reluctant, but she said OK. I gingerly took all the pins out and let her beautiful, magnificent silver tresses flow down her back.

And then I began asking questions. I asked her about what it was like being the eldest of four sisters. She told me that when she was barely three, her mother had another baby, and the baby was sick. Because her mother was having so much trouble managing a toddler and a sick newborn, she enrolled Asna in kindergarten two years early. Asna was very tall for her age, and registration in those days didn't require a birth certificate. So, since she looked older, they just took her, no questions asked. If they *had* asked any questions, they would have realized she didn't speak any English. In other words, not only was she taller than all the other kids and younger than all the other kids, but she spoke only Yiddish. And children being children, she was teased and bullied. And obviously it shaped her.

So her aloofness had nothing to do with me. It was a defense she had learned for her survival. But underneath I found a warm and receptive heart. After hearing that story, I fell in love with her, and from that moment on, whenever I was with her, I would just think about that three-year-old, and I would melt. And once I melted, surprise, surprise, she melted too.

It's the story that did it. When you find out that someone you can't stand was broken into little bitty pieces sitting at their dining room table, and you sat at your own table being broken, having your own innocence stolen from you, somehow the connection (if you can get out of your own preconceived way) becomes profoundly powerful. You can say inwardly, *Wow, you are me with an antique oak oblong table instead of a shiny brand-new mahogany rectangle table. But yes, we are the same.*

We all just want to be understood. We all just want to be loved. We all just want to be heard!

I'm hoping reading these different pieces, and writing some of your own, has reminded you that compassion has always been your first language. And hopefully these stories will help make you even more fluent.

The perpetrator in your story, the one who hurt you, can be called your own personal enemy. The Dalai Lama said, "We need enemies, and should be grateful to them. From the viewpoint of training in altruism, an enemy is really your guru, your teacher; only an enemy can teach you tolerance." My friend Margo calls them "your guru in drag." It's hard work to be grateful if someone hurt you. But what else are we doing here if not the hard work of becoming better, bigger, more loving beings? Writing essays is the best way I know of doing that work.

It's also a magical way of processing and healing grief.

Ram Dass said:

We're just faced with such a continuing barrage of suffering. And each time we form an attachment to another human being it is inevitable that sooner or later, one of you is going to die. So... in a way, the nature of attachment to human beings has loss built-in.

That's part of what makes life precious and frightening at the same moment.

Choosing to use grief as a healer takes time. And practice. And writing is a practice. And the thing is, you're not just healing yourself by writing your story. You are healing the reader. Because somewhere out there, there is someone with a wound the exact same shape as your words.

So give yourself and the world the gift of your essays. Keep writing. Keep loving. Keep being.

Because it's never too late to turn darkness into something close to dazzling light. Please, if you do anything with this book, use writing for the most important person in your story.

And that, dear beloved one, is *you*.

The Next Step

I have been listening to Deepak Chopra, and it's having a profound effect on my teaching and my own work on my own self.

The present moment. There's something to it. More than something. One of the things Chopra says is that our traumas are not who we are; they are just things that happened to us. He says we are all fictional characters in a collective dreamscape. Well, that's certainly another way to look at it.

I encourage you to write personal essays as a way of addressing your past struggles — the hurts, the slights, the slices to your perfect heart. This will empower you to remember, re-member, return, re-turn, to your compassionate self, your true nature.

And then, once the wounds have been written and have begun to heal, comes the freeing part: It's time to let go of that past and live in the perfection of the NOW. You'll know because you'll feel that the story you've been writing and rewriting is old. That maybe you have been loyal to your suffering. That it's time to let it go and move on. It may take decades. It may take writing the same prompt forty-seven times (like I did with "Dinner at our house was…"). It may not happen right away because you're still processing. Which is fine too.

Personally, I'm understanding "the present moment *is all there is*" more than I ever have. Between *Be Here Now* by Ram Dass, my teacher since 1977, Eckhart Tolle's *The Power of Now*, and Thich Nhat Hanh saying the present is the only thing there is, I'm wondering why it has taken me so long to get this. I should say, *is taking* me so long, because I'm still working at it. But it is so worth the work.

So when you get to that place where there's no more past and the future is unknown, and you've said bye-bye to the story that shaped you, what will you write about? Let's wait and see. Shall we wait together (in the moment)?

I think the title of my next book will be *PHEW!*

With love,
Nancy

Acknowledgments

My profound gratitude to all the contributors who shared their most intimate stories with me in the sacred circle of the Chilmark Writing Workshop. And to those who submitted your beautiful pieces but were not included in this edition, I thank you.

Thank you to my agent and friend, Flip Brophy.

Thanks to my adorable editor Jason Gardner. And special thanks to editor Kristen Cashman for her guidance, patience, and FaceTiming helping this Luddite look good. She didn't impose her voice — she used mine and made it better.

To my muses, my Tuesday writing group, the GGs, who have listened, suggested, edited, laughed, cried, and applauded every word I have written. I am in love with each one of you: Laura Roosevelt, Cathy Walthers, Nicole Galland, Lara O'Brien, and Kate Feiffer.

And to my precious friends and family who have held my heart during my hardest times: Alan Aronie, Emmanuel Aronie, Steve and Rose Aronie, Brooke Adams and Tony Shalhoub, Doreen Beinart, Nancy Berger, Connie Berry, Rabbis Caren Broitman and Brian Walt, Geraldine Brooks, Mirabai Bush, Adam Curtis, Ron Curtis, Michale Estar, Melinda and Peter Farrelly, Deb and Mirium Freed, Martha and Peter Halperin, Lorie and Richard Hamermesh, Judith Hannan, Caitlin Kane, Cindy Kane, Judith Kaufman and Steve Kemper, Jane Lancellotti, Elise Lebovit, David and Sharon Mann, Becky Minnich, Liz Moss, Debbie Phillips and Jim Murrin, Andrea and John Pitera, Jennifer Prax, Lissa Rankin and Jeff Rediger, Frannie Southworth, Mirabai Starr, Peter Stray, Kate Taylor, David and Merle Trager, Rabbi Tzvi and Hadassah Aperowitz, Liz Witham and Ken Wentworth, and the West Meadow Gang: Brooke and Michael Urban, Jane Rainwater and Ed Hogan, John Cooney, Malachy Duffy and Julie Hauserman. And to DeDe Lahman, my spiritual sister and teacher.

I thank my son Josh for feeding me in more ways than one.

And to my grandson, Eli — if he doesn't read anything else in this book, I hope he reads this page so he is reminded of how much I love him.

And to my spirit guides: my sister, Margie; my son Dan; and Hennie, my mommy, who was my first cheerleader.

Thank you to Ram Dass, who taught me to keep my heart open in hell.

And finally to my beloved Joel, who has consistently made that possible. And added heaven to the mix.

Endnotes

p. 8   *"Essayists tend to argue with themselves"*: Tracy Kidder and Richard Todd, *Good Prose: The Art of Nonfiction* (2013; repr., New York: Random House, 2015), 67.

p. 8   *"How do I know what I mean until I hear what I say?"*: Kidder and Todd, *Good Prose*, 72.

p. 30   *"For many, watching sports"* and *"Being a sports fan, it turns out"*: Abdo Elnakouri, "Is Being a Sports Fan a Waste of Time?," *Psychology Today* (blog), February 1, 2021, https://www.psychologytoday.com/us/blog/mind-large/202102/is-being-sports-fan-waste-time.

p. 41   *"Many of us are raised by well-intending parents"*: Mark Nepo, *The Book of Awakening, 20th Anniversary Edition* (Newburyport, MA: Red Wheel / Weiser, 202), 45.

p. 41   *"Nothing like a Republican convention to drive you screaming back"*: Molly Ivins, "Notes from Another Country," in *Nothin' but Good Times Ahead* (1993; repr., New York: Vintage, 1994), 135.

p. 42   *"Considering how common illness is"*: Virginia Woolf, *On Being Ill* (1930; repr., Middletown, CT: Wesleyan University Press, 2021), 3.

p. 108   *"Our lives are written in disappearing ink"*: Michelle Cliff, *The Store of a Million Items: Stories* (Boston: Houghton Mifflin, 1998), 22.

p. 165   *"but not necessarily in that order"*: David Sterritt, *The Films of Jean-Luc Godard: Seeing the Invisible* (Cambridge, UK: Cambridge University Press, 1999), 20.

p. 186   *"Almost everyone we knew landed on the same"*: Colin Campbell, "What Losing My Two Children Taught Me About Grief," *The Atlantic*, March 1, 2023, https://www.theatlantic.com/ideas/archive/2023/03/how-to-talk-about-grief-support/673232.

p. 204   *"Why so pale and wan fond lover?"*: Sir John Suckling, "Song: Why So

Pale and Wan Fond Lover?," Poetry Foundation, accessed May 29, 2024, https://www.poetryfoundation.org/poems/45247/song-why -so-pale-and-wan-fond-lover.

p. 215 *"We need enemies"*: Dalai Lama, *How to Expand Love: Widening the Circle of Loving Relationships* (New York: Atria, 2005), 63.

p. 215 *"We're just faced with such a continuing barrage"*: Ram Dass (@babaram dass), Instagram, November 13, 2023, https://www.instagram.com /babaramdass/reel/CzmCI9JxwRP.

Contributor Bios

JOHN ABRAMS cofounded Abrams Angell after fifty years as founder and president of South Mountain Company, a worker-owned B Corp. He blogs at AbramsAngell.com/blog, and he's working on a book called *Founder to Future: New Strategies for Business Impact, Equity, and Succession*. He misses his dad.

JUSTEN AHREN is the author of two collections of poetry, *A Strange Catechism* and *A Machine for Remembering*. Founder and director of Noepe Center for the Literary Arts, and Devotion to Writing, he lives on Martha's Vineyard.

GREG ANTON is best known as a San Francisco Bay Area drummer and composer. He's also a practicing attorney. *When Is More Important Than What* is a sequel to his first novel, *Face the Music* (Plus One Press, 2015). As an attorney, Greg has been a champion of medical marijuana rights. In 2015 Greg achieved a landmark federal court decision, which allowed medical marijuana to be distributed in California free of federal interference.

NAOMI BEINART is a fifteen-year-old writer who lives in New York City with her parents.

GLENN BERGENFIELD is the father of six, the husband of Sarah, a deprogrammed lawyer, and a Jewish guy who believes you never cut funny.

ELLENORA CAGE is a filmmaker, poet, and photographer who has turned her lens on fiction and memoir in the past few years. Her work has been published in the literary magazines *Bombay Gin* and *Narrative*, and her short story "The Sound of Snow" was made into an episode of the podcast *The Strange Recital*.

JAN COOK CHAPMAN is a journalist for print and television and is working on her fourth novel.

KATE FEIFFER is the author of eleven books for children, including *Henry the Dog with No Tail* and *My Mom Is Trying to Ruin My Life*. She also paints, draws, cartoons, and doodles and is the event producer for the writer's festival Islanders Write. *Morning Pages*, her first novel for adults, was published by Regalo Press in 2024.

DAPHNE FREISE left her childhood home in the Midwest and spent thirty years as a flight attendant. She and her husband live in Pennsylvania, where she is writing memoirs about her worldwide travels and her family's brush with a convicted mafia hit man.

NICOLE GALLAND is a bestselling novelist, writing teacher, and theater artist who divides her time between Massachusetts, Ireland, and several imaginary worlds. She loves Shakespeare, dogs, and functional democracies.

PHEBE GRANDISON is a sophomore at Oberlin College. She loves to create imaginary worlds and write fantasy, though she dabbles in poetry and personal essays as well.

KATHY GUNST is a James Beard Award–winning food journalist. She is the resident chef for NPR's award-winning show *Here & Now*, heard on over 550 public radio stations. She writes for *The Washington Post*, *Cognoscenti*, *Yankee*, *Eating Well*, and other publications. She teaches a writing workshop called "Finding Voice in

Food and Memoir Writing" all over the globe. She lives in southern Maine.

BRAD HAMERMESH is a senior at Needham High School in Needham, Massachusetts.

JUDITH HANNAN is a writer of memoir (*Motherhood Exaggerated*), essays, and short stories. Through her teaching, she is an activist in the healing power of writing for those affected by illness, for medical professionals, and for those affected negatively by society's disparities.

SUSAN JOYNER is a silver-haired gal from North Carolina who loves kicking pine cones and doesn't own china.

STEVE KEMPER has written four books of nonfiction and many articles for national publications. His website is SteveKemper.net.

JULIA KIDD is a psychotherapist, artist, and writer who lives and works on Martha's Vineyard. Her personal essays are often humorous, sometimes biting, but always rich with themes of popular culture, relationships, and the desire to be known.

NANCY KRAMER is an entrepreneur, chief evangelist at IBM, and an engaged mother and grandmother. She and her husband, fellow entrepreneur Christopher Celeste, and their barely obedient mastiff-Lab, Oggie, split time between Ohio and their beloved Martha's Vineyard.

DEDE LAHMAN is a restaurateur and coauthor of *The Clinton St. Baking Company Cookbook: Breakfast, Brunch & Beyond from New York's Favorite Neighborhood Restaurant* (Little, Brown, 2010). Before joining the restaurant life, she worked for a decade as an editor and writer for national magazines.

JANE LANCELLOTTI received a 2017 Pushcart Prize for her essay "If You Can't Say Anything Nice, Write a One-Star Review." A 2015 graduate of the Sarah Lawrence MFA Program, she is Readers' Narratives editor at *Narrative* magazine. During her advertising career, she worked on more than two hundred products for Saatchi & Saatchi New York. Her most notable work was seen on MTV for "Rock the Vote." She is married and has one daughter.

LAURA LENTZ is a writer, editor, and creative coach. She is the author of *STORYquest: The Writer, the Hero, the Journey*. She runs writing workshops online and retreats on Kauai, Hawaii.

ELIZABETH LESSER is the author of several bestselling books, including *Cassandra Speaks: When Women are the Storytellers, the Human Story Changes* and *Broken Open: How Difficult Times Can Help Us Grow*. She is the cofounder of Omega Institute and is one of Oprah Winfrey's Super Soul 100, a collection of a hundred leaders who are using their voices and talent to elevate humanity.

TAFFY MCCARTHY is an actor, singer, and theater director. She is a graduate of Goddard College, where she wrote, created, and performed a one-woman show called *I Know You Are but What Am I?* She continues to write and fall in love with her family, keeping them alive on the page and in her heart.

COLIN MCENROE writes a weekly column that runs in eight Hearst publications and hosts a radio show on Connecticut Public Radio.

ABIGAIL MCGRATH is the founder of Renaissance House, a retreat for writers of poetry and social issues. She created Renaissance House in memory of her mother, the poet Helene Johnson, and her aunt, Dorothy West, the novelist, both "Renaissance Women."

Retired, TERRY MCGUIRE now writes mainly fiction. Her favorite characters in books and life are quirky, imaginative, and quick to laugh. She lives on the Connecticut shoreline, near family and friends.

PETER MEYER, formerly a special-needs attorney advocating for youth with learning differences, is now a life coach and writer. He, his wife, and their four children all live in greater Burlington, Vermont.

JIM MURRIN is an award-winning artist who spent forty years as an endodontist, and on occasion his patients were tigers, bears, and gorillas in need of root canals.

HOLLY NADLER has been a professional writer since 1970, when she was invited to join the Writers Guild of America. She has published books of local Martha's Vineyard interest and thousands of newspaper and magazine articles, a few in national publications such as *Lear's*, *Women's World*, and *Cosmopolitan*.

LARA O'BRIEN is the founder of Howth Writing Workshop and Hooks & Reels literary and Irish musical performance events. She is based in Howth, Ireland, and Vinalhaven, Maine.

BARBARA PHILLIPS, a social justice feminist with essays in *Southern Cultures*, *The New York Times*, *HerStory*, *The Sun*, *Citron Review*, and elsewhere, lives in Oxford, Mississippi.

DR. BEVERLY PINCUS is a licensed clinical psychologist with expertise in trauma treatment and cross-cultural psychology, and a writer of personal essay and poetry. She is a social justice activist who provides pro bono psychological evaluations for asylum through Physicians for Human Rights and represents her congregation on the Synagogue Coalition on the Refugee and Immigration Crisis (SCRIC).

LINDA PEARCE PRESTLEY is a retired judge, an adoptive parent, and mom of way too many kids.

LISSA RANKIN, MD, is a mind-body medicine physician and expert in trauma-informed medicine, the author of seven books, and founder of the Whole Health Medicine Institute training program for physicians, as well as the nonprofit Heal At Last. Her TEDx Talks have been viewed over six million times, and she starred in two national public television specials.

JOY REICHART is a writer and coach who holds gentle space for genuine expression. She's the founder of Soul Writing, an organization that helps writers from all backgrounds and levels of experience get the words flowing, and the author of *Soul Writing: Connecting to Essence*. She's based in Berkeley, California, and works with folks worldwide. More at SoulWriting.org.

LAURA D. ROOSEVELT is a freelance journalist, poet, and copy editor whose published work has included numerous personal essays. She is currently working on a memoir. She lives on Martha's Vineyard.

Since 1957 BRADFORD ROWE has been evolving into a true Renaissance man — a poet, artist, musician, storyteller, and plumber. His second book, *Since Then*, is due out in 2024. He's presently morphing in Plymouth, Massachusetts.

SUZANNE A. SEGGERMAN is working on a true-crime book, *Imperfect Monsters: A Tale of Family, Wealth, and Vengeance*.

TONY SHALHOUB is an award-winning actor and writer.

MIRABAI STARR is an award-winning author of creative nonfiction and contemporary translations of sacred literature. She taught philosophy and world religions at the University of New Mexico–Taos for twenty years and now teaches and speaks internationally on contemplative practice and inter-spiritual dialogue. A certified bereavement counselor, Mirabai helps mourners harness the transformational power of loss. Her latest book, *Wild Mercy: Living the Fierce and Tender Wisdom of the Women Mystics*, was named one of the "Best Books of 2019." She lives with her extended family in the mountains of northern New Mexico.

KATE TAYLOR is a singer, songwriter, artist, craftsperson, mother, and grandmother. She lives year-round on Martha's Vineyard. She was raised in Chapel Hill, North Carolina. Her brothers Alex, James, Livingston, and Hugh are also songwriters and performers.

A native of Nashville, SUZY TROTTA lives in Knoxville, Tennessee, with her husband and their four-legged fur babies. She earned a master's degree in German, which is why she sold real estate for twenty years. She is the author of the upcoming book *Open House: Mostly True Tales of Crazy in Southern Real Estate* from Howling Hills Publishing.

CATHERINE WALTHERS is a chef and the author of four cook-books, including her latest, *Kale, Glorious Kale*. She graduated from the chef's program at the Natural Gourmet Institute in New York City and works as a private chef in Boston and Martha's Vine-yard and as food editor for *Bluedot Living*, a national climate change magazine and website.

JUDITH HANNAH WEISS wrote for clients like Time Warner and Condé Nast. Then she got hit by a drunk with a truck, which put a few things on hold. Post-truck work has appeared in *Oldster*, *Salmagundi*, *The Rumpus*, *Dorothy Parker's Ashes*, *The Iowa Review*, and many others. She lives near Charlottesville, Virginia, where she also makes art for humans and homes for birds.

GERALD YUKEVICH (pen name: Ivan Cox; author website: Ivan Cox.com) lives and practices medicine on Martha's Vineyard. He writes essays and screenplays, and his two novels are *Cruise Ship Doctor* and *Blood Pudding*.

About the Author

Nancy Slonim Aronie is the founder of the Chilmark Writing Workshop on Martha's Vineyard, a multiday experience that she offers several times a year, and author of *Memoir as Medicine* and *Writing from the Heart*. She was a commentator for National Public Radio's *All Things Considered*, a monthly columnist for *McCall's* magazine, a feature writer for *Lear's* magazine, a visiting writer at Trinity College in Hartford, Connecticut, and a recipient of the Eye of the Beholder Artist in Residence Award at the Isabella Stewart Gardner Museum in Boston. She was recognized for excellence in teaching for all three years she taught with Robert Coles at Harvard University. Nancy teaches Jump-Start Your Memoir and Write It from the Heart at Esalen Institute, Kripalu Center for Yoga and Health, Omega Institute, New York Open Center, and Blue Spirit Costa Rica. Her column "From the Heart" appears biweekly in *The Martha's Vineyard Times*.

ChilmarkWritingWorkshop.com

NEW WORLD LIBRARY is dedicated to publishing books and other media that inspire and challenge us to improve the quality of our lives and the world.

We are a socially and environmentally aware company. We recognize that we have an ethical responsibility to our readers, our authors, our staff members, and our planet.

We serve our readers by creating the finest publications possible on personal growth, creativity, spirituality, wellness, and other areas of emerging importance. We serve our authors by working with them to produce and promote quality books that reach a wide audience. We serve New World Library employees with generous benefits, significant profit sharing, and constant encouragement to pursue their most expansive dreams.

We print our books with soy-based ink on paper from sustainably managed forests. We power our Northern California office with solar energy, and we respectfully acknowledge that it is located on the ancestral lands of the Coast Miwok Indians. We also contribute to nonprofit organizations working to make the world a better place for us all.

Our products are available wherever books are sold.

customerservice@NewWorldLibrary.com
Phone: 415-884-2100 or 800-972-6657
Orders: Ext. 110
Fax: 415-884-2199
NewWorldLibrary.com

Scan below to access our newsletter
and learn more about our books and authors.